NUCLEAR DISARMAMENT:

INDIA-E.U. PERSPECTIVES

Editor
V .R. Raghavan

DPG

DELHI POLICY GROUP   **VIJ BOOKS INDIA PVT LTD**

Published by

Vij Books India Pvt Ltd

2/19, Ansari Road, Darya Ganj
New Delhi - 110002
Phones: 91-11-65449971, 91-11- 43596460
Fax: 91-11-47340674
e-mail : vijbooks@rediffmail.com
web : www.vijbooks.com

ISBN 13 : 978-93-80177-44-1

CONTENTS

INTRODUCTION

India's acquiring of nuclear weapons led to many outcomes since 1998. The expected ones were the sanctions imposed on it by almost all developed countries, including from Europe. The degree or intensity of sanctions were influenced by the states' perceptions of their future relations with India, including economic and defence relations. The latter involved the sale of military hardware to one of the world's largest defence markets. This was indicative of their perceptions of both, nuclear proliferation and disarmament. It took less than five years for India's nuclear weapons to be seen as a stabilising element in global and regional security calculations. The war in Kargil in 1999 and India's legislation on technology control measures on nuclear issues helped in creating this new perception. The beginning of new strategic relations with the US made a significant impact on perceptions of nuclear India. Its willingness to abide by the IAEA's verification regime, and the acceptance of Nuclear Supplier Group demands greatly helped in the new outlook. Indian economic growth, its nuclear energy needs and increasing role in the global scene provided the overarching environment in which a new outlook on a nuclear India has crystallised.

Nuclear deterrence inevitably became an issue in Indian thinking. Not long after acquiring nuclear weapons, India produced a nuclear doctrine which added to perceptions of India's responsible approach on deterrence. The principal Indian doctrinal element was of *No First Use*. This was supplemented by the policy of Minimum Credible Deterrence which effectively placed India out of a nuclear arms race.

Indian policy on nuclear disarmament on the other hand, has been one of long standing support and approval of measures leading to it. The first decade of 21st century has seen a resurgence of support for global nuclear disarmament. The cascade of nuclear disarmament proposals has emerged from different sources. The Weapons of Mass Destruction Commission led by Hans Blix had produced a report with a set of recommendations. It was followed by the International Commission on Nuclear Non-Proliferation & Disarmament brought into being by the Australian and Japanese governments. In 2008, the European Union had outlined an Eight Point initiative to the then UN Secretary General. The same year, UN Secretary General Ban Ki Moon had delivered a major and meaningful address on nuclear disarmament. It was the first ever such address by a UN Secretary General exclusively on disarmament.

These initiatives take the nuclear disarmament discourse well beyond the earlier attempts of the 1990s. The "13 Practical Steps" on the implementing of Article VI of the NPT, resolutions offered by Japan, Myanmar, the New Agenda Coalition, all form part of disarmament proposals before the turn of the century. India, on its part had presented a Working Paper at the UNGA in 2006 that encapsulated a set of proposals that could lead to the elimination of nuclear weapons which form a part of its policy on the subject. Furthermore, the Statement by India's Representative at the UN Conference on Disarmament in Geneva had presented a seven-point approach to a world without nuclear weapons. In fact, these seven steps even have parallels to the four horsemen's action plan, primarily in terms of the reduction of the salience of nuclear weapons in the security doctrine. The cumulative impact of these disarmament ideas and proposals has been to throw up fresh questions on the relevance of nuclear deterrence and utility of nuclear weapons to the new types of threats faced by states today.

The Indian position has been clearly influenced by the current state and the history of developments in its neighbourhood, and the larger theatre of the Asia-Pacific as they pertain to nuclear issues. In the West, and especially among advocates of the arms control and non-proliferation approach, India is often criticized for focusing too much on the inequities of the arms control order rather than on using arms control as a building block towards nuclear disarmament. Yet, it must be noted that for India disarmament has always been a preferred moral position based in the belief that it cannot be achieved without nuclear arms control working coterminously. Indian opposition to the NPT and other treaties should be best understood in this context.

India is evidently committed to global nuclear disarmament and Indian strategists feel it is in India's strategic interest to have a world free of nuclear weapons. Indian strategists have watched with interest the evolving outlook on the subject from both nuclear weapon states and non-nuclear weapon states. In this strategically important debate the position of Europe is of particular interest. There are states in Europe which are nuclear while there are others who are not only non-nuclear, but also have a unique position on nuclear issues like extended deterrence. Within NATO there are differing opinions on the subject. Within the EU and NATO there are states which have joined from the erstwhile Soviet bloc and Warsaw pact.

There has been little interaction between India and Europe on nuclear issues. The seminar on *Nuclear Non-Proliferation and Disarmament* held in June 2010 in New Delhi was one such attempt to build awareness on Indian and European perspectives on nuclear disarmament. In its examination it was observed that the position of Germany and Poland were of special interest to the discourse. The German position over the year on nuclear weapons proved to be a remarkable demonstration of strategic vision and alliance pragmatism. It was a major player during the Cold War on tactical nuclear weapons and its strong position on the subject had in no small measure resulted in the INF Treaty. After the end of Cold War, it has restructured its relations with Russia and the location on its borders of states like Poland has been watched with interest. German energy needs offer a strategic compulsion for the future. Its emerging set of energy flow arrangements with Russia and its simultaneous need to balance that with European neighbours makes a fascinating study. Dr. Harald Muller, the noted German scholar's paper, offers an excellent analysis of German nuclear perspectives and dilemmas. The seminar participants gained immensely from his presentation.

Poland has been both a partner in and a victim of German and Russian empires. Its current independent status bordering both these states marks a unique turn in its history. Therfore, its position on nuclear weapons and disarmament offers an insight into a new European outlook. The introduction of ABMs in

Poland recently evoked strong response from Russia. This U.S initiative has spin-off effects beyond Poland and Russia. Dr. Lukas Kulesa from Poland provided a fine analysis of his country's views on nuclear disarmament.

Indian strategic analysts at the seminar, included Ambassador Arundhati Ghosh, Prof. Rajesh Rajagopalan, and Brig. Gurmeet Kanwal. Their papers offer a detailed analysis of the Indian disarmament debate. Mr. K Subrahmanyam, Dr. C Raja Mohan, former Foreign Secretary, Kanwal Sibal, among others offered significant insights into Indian strategic needs and disarmament dilemmas.

The seminar was supported by the Hanns Seidel Foundation. The Delhi Policy Group is happy to acknowledge the valuable support in making the path breaking seminar a reality.

November 2010
Delhi Policy Group

V.R. Raghavan

INDIA, THE NPT AND DISARMAMENT: DISJUNCTION OR CONVERGENCE?

Arundhati Ghose

"When we are talking, therefore, of non-proliferation...we are talking of proliferation of nuclear weapons not of the proliferation of a so-called closed club...A non-proliferation agreement is, therefore, basically an agreement to be entered into by the nuclear powers not to proliferate nuclear weapons." [1]

Statement by Ambassador V.C. Trivedi to the Eighteen Nation Disarmament Committee, 12 August 1965

I : Disjunction

The disjunction between India and the Treaty on the Non-Proliferation of Nuclear Weapons emerged at the inception of the negotiations of the Treaty and increased till India was unable in her interests to even consider joining the NPT. As a result, Treaty supporters and India either ignored each other at best, or

---

[1] Statement b y Ambassador V .C.Trivedito the Eighteen Nation Disarmament Committee (ENDC) on 12 August 1965; 'Documents on India's Nuclear Disarmament Policy', Vol I p.590

were virulently adversarial at worst. The core of the disjunction was the issue of nuclear disarmament. Today, an interesting opportunity for convergence has appeared, if not on the wording of the Treaty itself, on its objectives and principles, and most importantly, on the implementation of measures to attain those objectives. To more clearly understand and appreciate India's positions, both on the NPT and on the issue of nuclear disarmament, it is necessary to briefly revisit the history of India's engagement in the negotiations that led to the ultimate adoption of the Treaty and therefore, the context of India's approach to both non-proliferation and disarmament, and in a sense to the issue of nuclear weapons.

From the outset, India viewed nuclear weapons as a threat to India's own security, and to international stability. Prime Minister Jawaharlal Nehru wrote in 1954 that these new weapons would cause fear to "grow and grip nations and peoples, and each would try frantically to get this new weapon or some adequate protection from it,"[2] Nehru recognized that "a dominating factor in the modern world is this prospect of these terrible weapons suddenly coming into use before which our normal weapons are completely useless."[3] Nehru also believed in the ability of nuclear power being able and therefore, necessary to solve the challenges of development with which as a newly independent country India was faced. India, therefore started to campaign for disarmament, signed the Partial Test Ban Treaty in 1963, and entered into an agreement with the United States on cooperation in civilian nuclear energy. However, in October 1964, almost two years to

---

[2] Jawaharlal Nehru: "The Death Dealer" National Herald 2 April 1954

[3] Speech by Jawaharlal Nehru to the Conference of Scientists on Deve   lopment of Atomic Energy for Peaceful Purposes 26 November 1954

the day that India was defeated in a border war with China, China conducted its first nuclear test; there was great domestic pressure on the Indian Government to move down the path towards weaponisation. Nehru was dead and India decided to go instead to the United Nations in the hope that international pressure on China would prevent it from becoming a full-fledged nuclear weapon State and that non-nuclear weapon States would receive guarantees from the UN against any nuclear threat or coercion. Using the good offices of the Soviet Union, India was able to inscribe on the agenda of the UN General Assembly, the issue of proliferation.

Early in 1965, at the UN Disarmament Commission, discussions turned to the consideration of a treaty or convention to prevent the proliferation of nuclear weapons. The Indian delegate proposed a 'comprehensive proposal' based on five principles introducing the concept of 'balance' as the basis of any future treaty. The nuclear weapon powers were to undertake:

- Not to transfer nuclear weapons or nuclear weapons technology to others;

- Nuclear powers should agree not to use nuclear weapons against countries that did not possess them;

- The UN must safeguard the security of countries which may be threatened by nuclear weapon states or states near to possessing nuclear weapons';

- There should be tangible progress toward disarmament, including a comprehensive test ban treaty, a complete freeze on the production of nuclear weapons and means of delivery as well as substantial reduction in the existing stocks; and

- It should be a Treaty committing non-nuclear powers not to acquire or manufacture nuclear weapons.

Clearly, India was seeking some sort of protection against a possible Chinese nuclear threat. This remained India's basic brief during the negotiations. As noted by George Perkovich, "American and Indian visions of an effective non-proliferation treaty formed the parameters of the debate with the other nations in between."[4] During the UN General Assembly that year, India, together with seven other countries (Brazil, Burma, Ethiopia, Mexico, Nigeria, Sweden and the United Arab Republic (Egypt) presented a memorandum which stated that "measures to prohibit the spread of nuclear weapons should be coupled with or followed by, tangible steps to halt the nuclear arms race and to limit, reduce and eliminate the stocks of nuclear weapons and their means of delivery."[5] That General Assembly adopted Resolution 2828(XX), which formed the mandate to negotiate a non-proliferation treaty and which, *inter alia*, said:

(a) The Treaty should be void of any loopholes which might permit nuclear or non-nuclear powers to proliferate, directly or indirectly, nuclear weapons in any form;

(b) The Treaty should embody an acceptable balance of mutual responsibilities and obligations of the nuclear and non-nuclear powers.

The resolution was adopted with no votes against, and five abstentions.

---

[4] George Perkovich: India's Nuclear Bomb:The Impact on Global Proliferation 1999 p.103

[5] Documentson India's Disarmament Policy:Vol. II p.602

Disarmament was clearly the priority area for the international community at that time. However, it was the height of the Cold War and the memories in Europe of the last War were still fairly fresh. Through what has been called a careful "management of alliances" [6] the NPT as it finally emerged was not meant to be a disarmament treaty at all. Disarmament was recognized as a desirable objective, and nuclear weapon states were committed only to "negotiations in good faith" to stop the arms race and to nuclear disarmament. Alliance partners of both super powers were extended the nuclear umbrella, and, in some cases with the weapons located on the territories of, and till the 1970s, under the control of the host, purportedly non-nuclear countries. The NPT, and non-proliferation became synonymous with the control of the spread of nuclear weapons to states other than those in alliance to the super powers, rather than including prohibitions on the increase in the number of nuclear weapons already in existence.

To return to the negotiations: India had another priority in her vision of the new Treaty, and that was to ensure that it did not discriminate against the non-nuclear weapon states, of which she was one. There is no doubt that the demand for equality was based not only on ethical grounds and from the point of view of a post-colonial history, but also to keep the field open for non-nuclear weapon states to keep open the option to weaponise, if the nuclear weapon states did not disarm. This was, in a sense, a reflection of an Italian proposal that non-nuclear weapon states agree not to weaponise for a given period of time. In the event of the nuclear weapon states failing to fulfill their commitment to

---

[6] K.Subrahmanyam: various references, including to the author

disarmament, those non-nuclear weapon states that wished to develop these weapons for their security purposes would be free to do so. In May 1967, when the then two super powers started their bilateral negotiations on their respective drafts, the Indian delegate enunciated what could be taken to represent the Indian position on the Treaty for the next several decades. It is worthwhile to quote him in some detail. Speaking to the ENDC, Ambassador Trivedi said: "Even apart from measures of disarmament, however, the very facts of political life of today demand that nations, and particularly a nation like India, which is exposed to nuclear black mail, take full account of the needs of national security...the great powers have (held) that they cannot accept this or that proposal of nuclear restraint or reduction because it would adversely affect their security. But, when they address themselves to non-nuclear, powers, the nuclear weapon powers argue that nuclear weapons provide no security and that the best way the non-nuclear nations can safeguard their security is to sign a discriminatory treaty-a treaty which will at the same time give unfettered license to five powers to proliferate...It is a matter of vital concern to India, that one of the lesser nuclear powers, in particular, is feverishly building up its arsenal of weapons and developing its delivery capability."[7] This, of course, was a direct reference to the threat perception India sensed from China; the reason she had brought the issue of non-proliferation to the UN in the first place.

At the same time, it would be an error to imagine that the ethical or moral argument against nuclear weapons was totally absent. The pursuit of security imperatives without any sort of moral grounding would have been seen as unacceptable by

---

[7] Statement by Ambassador V.K.Trivedi to the ENDC on 23 May 1967.Documents on India's Nuclear Disarmament Policy Vol. II pp. 696-697

countries like India that were either non-aligned or neutral in the context of Cold War politics.

In the event, India lost on all counts; as a non-nuclear state she received no security assurances, not even when she tried to do so bilaterally, there was little emphasis on the 'balance' she had demanded in the obligations of those countries with nuclear weapons and those without, disarmament became a 'pipe dream' as seen by a US negotiator three decades later, and China became authorized to possess and increase her nuclear arsenal, even though she did not sign the Treaty till 1992. As George Perkovich says: "India may have had logic, principle and the 1965 mandate on her side, but the United States and the other nuclear powers had power on their side."[8]

Yet, it needs to be noted that when Mrs. Indira Gandhi informed the Lok Sabha in April 1968 of India's decision to reject the Treaty, she not only said that in rejecting the Treaty, "we shall be guided entirely by our enlightened self-interest and the considerations of national security...(even though non-signature) may mean the stoppage of aid (and) may involve sacrifice and hardship, it will be the first step towards building the real strength of this country.." but she reiterated India's decision not to manufacture nuclear weapons herself.[9] Instead, India pushed ahead with renewed vigour in all available forums, to not just criticize the NPT, but to promote the cause of nuclear disarmament. India became, for all practical purposes, a part of the so-called 'disarmament lobby'.

---

[8] Perkovich (ibid) p.127
[9] Indira Gandhi: Debate on Foreign Affairs, Lok Sabha, New Delhi, 5 April 1968

Almost in a parallel narrative, the five yearly Review Conferences of the NPT were held, restrictions on non-nuclear weapon states were tightened, India conducted a peaceful nuclear experiment in 1974, suffered sanctions (though in her view she had broken no laws)and the abrogation of the first US-India Agreement on Civil Nuclear cooperation and the disruption of the international cooperation on the basis of which she was hoping to meet her developmental challenges took place. The disjunction was complete.

India did not attend any of the Review meetings and used the Non-Aligned forum and the UN General Assembly to put forward her ideas on disarmament, including the Rajiv Gandhi Action Plan for ushering in a Nuclear Weapon Free and non-violent World Order.[10] This Action Plan not only offered once again, in return for tangible steps towards disarmament by the nuclear weapon States, a 'balance' with non-nuclear Weapon States undertaking "not to cross the threshold into the acquisition of nuclear Weapons", but also promoted the idea of "a new Treaty eliminating all nuclear weapons by the year 2010 to replace the non-proliferation treaty (NPT)." The Action Plan and India were ignored as much as India continued to ignore the NPT. Even in the IAEA, where India is a founding member, India was careful to ensure that in all decisions, a separate category of countries, 'those not members of the NPT', was recognized. This situation continued till the 1995 Review Conference of the NPT, where it was decided that the NPT would be extended 'indefinitely'. This decision had a serious impact on India's negotiating position in the CTBT negotiations then underway in Geneva, and partially contributed to India's rejection of that Treaty, too. Inevitably,

---

[10] Towards a Nuclear Weapon Free World, Appendix 2 Ed.Manpreet Sethi 2009.

the results of the CTBT negotiations and confirmation of information of China's assistance to Pakistan, with which India had by that time fought three wars to build up a nuclear weapons arsenal, led to India's nuclear weapon tests in May 1998 and her declaration of herself as a country with nuclear weapons. As a consequence, India, which had begun to open up her economy to the global economy faced both, virulent condemnation and stringent sanctions on international trade and financial and technology flows. So great was the anger of the existing nuclear weapon powers, that the UN Security Council adopted Resolution 1172, condemning both India and Pakistan for having carried out the tests and called for both countries to immediately join the NPT as non-nuclear weapon states. (Pakistan, which had already as is now known carried out a nuclear test in 1990 in the Lop Nor test site in China, had, within two weeks of India's tests, carried out six of its own tests and also, in its usual "me too" routine, declared itself a nuclear weapon state.)

II : India and the NPT community consider shifts in position

"Although disarmament must remain the higher goal for which India needs to strive, the immediate aim of New Delhi after Pokhran II has been finding a modus Vivendi with the global nuclear order and participating in the many nuclear arms control agreements that seek partial rather than total solutions to the nuclear problem." [11]

Ironically, it was this period which saw the beginnings of a change in India's relations, if not with the NPT community then with most major powers, particularly the United States and Europe

---

[11] C.RajaMohan: Crossing the Rubicon: The shaping of India's New Foreign Policy 2003 p.15

which were staunch supporters, indeed, leaders, in the effort to promote the NPT as the international norm against proliferation of nuclear weapons to states other than the five permanent members of the UN Security Council. Perhaps optimistically, assured of her security concerns from nuclear weapons, two of India's Foreign Ministers, from two different parties, publicly and specifically stated India's support for the principles and objectives of the NPT, as a nuclear weapon state. India entered into intense discussions with the United States which had, as its focus, in a sense, not just India's relationship with the US, but also the relationship between India, the NPT and the NPT community. At issue were the sanctions that had been imposed on India, India's accession to the CTBT, cooperation on negotiating an FMCT and, in the interim, a moratorium on fissile material production, a limitation on the types of ballistic missiles India would develop and non-deployment of the ones already in India's arsenal, export controls and a dialogue with Pakistan. Much of this was based on a P-5 communique issued on June 4, immediately after the tests in 1998. There was no expectation by the US that India would even consider signing the NPT. Though the bilateral discussions did not have any concrete results, they did impact on the attitude of several European countries towards a nuclear armed India. The fact that India's market was expanding was perhaps an additional incentive. As noted by Strobe Talbott, "With every passing month, the US Congress was more impatient to lift the remaining sanctions. The administration faced the same problem with several foreign partners, especially fellow nuclear weapon states. Of the seven governments in the G-8 that had the power to continue blocking international lending to India, the administration had solid support only from the Japanese and the Canadians. The French (and the Italians) "portraying themselves as more understanding of India's security concerns than the Americans, dangled the possibility that India might, with French help, become eligible for nuclear assistance of the kind forbidden to non-NPT states,"[12] This ban on cooperation with non-NPT states in civil nuclear energy does not, of course exist in the NPT itself; it is a guideline adopted by the Nuclear Suppliers Group set up after India's 1974 test. Continuing, Talbott says: "Seeing France and Italy breaking ranks, the United Kingdom and Germany showed signs of being tempted to step up the pace of restoring to normal their own relations with India."[13]

It is not intended to describe the evolution of India-US relations nor to elaborate on the changes in India's nuclear and foreign policy, though these developments were crucial to the growing convergence between India and the non-proliferation regime. The purpose is to identify the gradual shift in positions of India on the one hand, and the NPT community on the other, on the issue of nuclear disarmament, since nuclear disarmament was the cause of the disjunction as described above. It has to be remarked, however, that in the India-US discussions, disarmament did not occur as an issue; yet, almost with the announcement of the nuclear tests in 1998, India reiterated her commitment to nuclear disarmament as an ultimate objective. In 1999, India's National Security Advisory Board produced a draft Nuclear Doctrine[14]; in its preamble, it refers to the permanent extension of the Nuclear Non-Proliferation Treaty (NPT) in 1995 which

---

[12] Strobe Talbott: Engaging India: Diplomacy, Democracy and the B omb: 2004 pp.142-143

[13] Ibid

[14] Draft Report of National Advisory Board on Indian Nuclear Doctrine: Nuclear Strategy: Manpreet Sethi: Appendix 1

sought to legitimize, on a selective basis the possession of nuclear weapons. "Nuclear weapon States have asserted that they will continue to rely on nuclear weapons with some of them adopting policies to use them even in a non-nuclear context. These developments amount to virtual abandonment of nuclear disarmament. This is a serious setback to the struggle of the international community to abolish weapons of mass destruction...(this) constitutes a threat to peace and stability." The draft doctrine contains a separate section on 'Disarmament and Arms Control'. Two of the noteworthy paragraphs of that section are :

"8.1. Global, verifiable and non-discriminatory nuclear disarmament is a national security objective. India shall continue its efforts to achieve the goal of a nuclear weapon-free world at an early date.

8.4. Nuclear arms control measures shall be sought as part of national security policy to reduce potential threats and to protect our own capability and its effectiveness."

In 2003, the Cabinet Committee on Security, in reviewing the operationalization of the doctrine, underlined that India's nuclear doctrine included "(viii) Continued commitment to the goal of a nuclear weapon-free world, through global, verifiable and non-discriminatory nuclear disarmament."[15] In a sense, this was India's answer to some of the criticisms raised by the NPT community after the Pokhran II tests and a statement of belief, which will need to be examined later.

---

[15] The Cabinet Committee on Security Reviews Operationalization of India's Nuclear Doctrine: Ibid : Appendix 2

In the meanwhile, India and the US had entered into a process known as the Next Steps in Strategic Partnership, where nuclear issues were also discussed. The NPT and nuclear disarmament issues were not on the table, and by the time Prime Minister Manmohan Singh and President George Bush issued a Joint statement on building closer bilateral relations, including "full civil nuclear energy cooperation" with India, the issue of both India signing the NPT or of the US committing itself to nuclear disarmament had faded from the scene, at least from bilateral relations. The two leaders did, however agree "that their countries would play a leading role in international efforts to prevent the proliferation of weapons of mass destruction, including nuclear, chemical, biological and radiological weapons."[16] This was a long way from the stands taken during the negotiation of the NPT.

In September 2008, with the support of the US and countries like France and Russia, the Nuclear Suppliers Group made an exception to their guideline regarding civilian cooperation with non-NPT states for India. The route to this historic agreement was turbulent and controversial, with several members of the NPT community being of the view that this 'exceptionalisation' of India would weaken the NPT and its regime. Yet, India agreed, for the first time, to place her civilian nuclear facilities under IAEA safeguards, including those that had been indigenously designed and built, agreed to bring her export control rules in line with those of the NSG and the Missile Technology Control Regime and signed an Additional Protocol with the IAEA. Without signing the NPT, India has brought most of her policies in line with those of the NPT, including

---

[16] India-US Joint Statement July 18, 2005 Ibid Appendix 3

negative security assurances to non-nuclear weapon states and recognition of nuclear weapon free zones as being important steps towards nuclear disarmament, a change from her earlier more skeptical attitude towards these zones.

On February 28th 2008, the Indian delegate to the Conference on Disarmament once again presented a set of measures towards reaching a world free of nuclear weapons. The steps included an unequivocal commitment of all nuclear weapon states to the goal of complete elimination of nuclear weapons, the reduction of the salience of nuclear weapons in their security doctrines, adoption of measures by nuclear weapon states to reduce nuclear danger, including the risks of accidental nuclear war, de-alerting of nuclear weapons, a global agreement among nuclear weapon states on 'no-first-use' of nuclear weapons, negotiation of a universal and legally binding agreement on non-use of nuclear weapons against non-nuclear weapon states, negotiation of a Convention on prohibition of use or threat of use of nuclear weapons and negotiation of a Nuclear Weapons Convention 'prohibiting the development, production, stockpiling and use of nuclear weapons and on their destruction, leading to the global, non-discriminatory and verifiable elimination of nuclear weapons with a specified time frame.' The appointment of a Special Coordinator to work on a mandate for a possible Ad Hoc Committee on Nuclear Disarmament was also proposed.

III : Global developments and the 2010 NPT Review Conference

"Re-assertion of the vision of a world free of nuclear weapons and practical measures toward achieving that goal would be, and would be perceived as, a bold initiative consistent

with America's moral heritage. Without the bold vision, the actions required will not be perceived as fair or urgent. Without the actions, the vision will not be perceived as realistic or possible."[17]

The issue of nuclear disarmament has also recently, and perhaps for the first time, received focused global attention, particularly from the major nuclear weapon states, starting with the two letters to the Wall Street Journal by the Cold Warriors of the past, eminent statesmen from the US, Kissinger, Perry, Schultz and Nunn. Their letters led to a lot of activity in the non-governmental circuit, including the setting up of an independent Commission by Australia and Japan which, *inter alia*, also considered what the NPT regime should do to bring the three 'outliers'-India, Pakistan and Israel- into the NPT framework. The most significant developments, however have come from the US, under the leadership of its President.

In President Obama's speech[18] in Prague in April 2009, he announced his country's "commitment to seek the peace and security of a world without nuclear weapons." He also announced the "reduction of the role of nuclear weapons in (our) national security strategy, and urge(d) others to do the same." In the US Nuclear Posture Review that appeared earlier this year, it would appear that efforts have been made, in fact, to reduce the role of nuclear weapons in US nuclear security policy. Whether this is a sustainable and irreversible position is difficult to predict, but the intention and reasoning appear fairly coherent with the

---

[17] Article by George Schultz,William J. Perry, Henry A. Kissinger and Sam Nunn: Wall Street Journal January 4, 2007

[18] Speech by US President Obama at Prague,Czech Republic, April 5, 2009: http://www.white house.gov/the _press- office/

President's commitment. In another significant reference, President Obama said "The threat of global nuclear war has gone down, but the risk of a nuclear attack has gone up." He highlighted the dangers of nuclear terrorism which he termed "the most immediate and extreme threat to global security." Though President Obama identified the strengthening of the NPT "as a basis for cooperation", it constituted only one of the elements in the US "trajectory" towards nuclear disarmament. The NPT, it would appear would remain, for the US at least, a framework for controlling the spread of nuclear weapons to states other than those endorsed by the NPT. The Nuclear Security Summit held in Washington in 2010 was held outside the NPT framework and the 'outlier' countries were invited as participants. It would be important to watch how these structures, outside the NPT itself, would fare; there already exits UN Security Council Resolution 1540, the Proliferation Security Initiative and the Global Initiative to Combat Nuclear Terrorism (which Obama seems to have the intention to turn into 'durable international institutions' rather than as at present, 'coalitions of the willing') as additional structures to the NPT, with the participation of non-NPT countries as well. Disarmament, it would appear would, for the foreseeable future remain at the unilateral and bilateral levels; nonproliferation to states and other 'unauthorised' entities, not only to the NPT and its mechanisms, but to a wider multilateral regime made up of several other institutions, including a vastly strengthened IAEA. This approach has not yet been either spelt out clearly, nor its outlines accepted by the NPT community.

The other source of ambiguity in the global activities outlined above, is whether they were intended to ensure the success of the 2010 NPT Review Conference, and whether, particularly the issue of disarmament, would once again be placed on the back burner once the Review Conference was over. There is no doubt that there was great anxiety about the future of the NPT's continued relevance; however, as the only international Treaty on nuclear non-proliferation, its survival was seen to be essential for the international community. The achievement of agreement on final documents at the Review Conference was due, in no small degree, to the very real compromises that were worked out among those countries which continue to hold diametrically opposed views, including on disarmament. It needs to be pointed out here that there is no agreement among the P-5 on President Obama's approach to a nuclear weapon-free world. France has said so openly as has Russia, and China remains as opaque as ever. This difference in approach, and the US commitments to "extended deterrence" to its worried allies in Eastern Europe and East Asia, are reflected in a new caveat being added to the issue of disarmament. This was presaged in UN Security Council Resolution 1887,[19] which was adopted unanimously on 24 September 2009, under the Chairmanship of President Obama, as a 'stage setter' for the all-important Review Conference, and which concentrated on the non-proliferation aspects of the Treaty; the resolution resolved "to seek a safer world for all and to create conditions for a world without nuclear weapons, in accordance with the goals of the Treaty on the Non-Proliferation of Nuclear Weapons(NPT), in a way that promotes international stability and based on the principle of undiminished security for all." This formulation is repeated in all references to nuclear disarmament. While the formulation is not new, it was used in the 2000 Review Conference document as well, the repetition in the 2010

---

[19] UN Security Council Resolution 1887 : http://www.america.gov/st/texttransenglish/2009/September /20090924173226

documents, after the major build up and the rhetoric on nuclear disarmament, would have been the cause of some disappointment. Infact, in the 2010 documents, the formulation has been tweaked a bit, and it now reads, "in a way that promotes international stability, peace and security, and based on the principle of undiminished and increased security for all."[20]

With the debate on the feasibility of disarmament not yet settled, with many holding that nuclear weapons have contributed to peace and stability in the world and that disarmament would lead to diminished security especially of states with weaker conventional arsenals, the acceptance of this formulation has weakened the cause of disarmament at least within the framework of the NPT.

Of course, the conclusions and recommendations section of the document contains agreement on follow-up in the Conference on Disarmament, but only on a 'subsidiary body to deal with nuclear disarmament, within the context of an agreed, comprehensive and balanced Programme of Work.' Such a subsidiary body, without a clear mandate would have little meaning; the Conference on Disarmament (CD) is a negotiating body and the UN General Assembly would have to give it the mandate to start negotiations. Otherwise, the 'subsidiary body' would only be used for stock statement of positions and little else would be accomplished.

Finally, the Review Conference documents have dealt with the issue of the non-members to the NPT in a way which ensures

---

[20] 2010 Review Conference of the Parties to the Treaty on the Non-Proliferation of Nuclear Weapons: Draft Final Document: Conclusions and Recommendations for the follow-on actions.

that those countries would not only ignore the expressed desires of the NPT community, but would effectively prevent any cooperation between those three countries, including India, with the NPT and its supporters. Efforts of some more realistic non-governmental groups such as the Australia-Japan sponsored ICNND, George Perkovich and James Acton's study of the issue, would seem to not have been subject to any debate during the Review Conference. India is bound to find the separate section on South Asia in the Review document particularly offensive; the fragility of the moves towards convergence are likely to have been severely damaged.

IV : Future Trends

It is not remarkable that India has not formally commented on the results of the recently concluded NPT Review Conference, nor that the issues of non-proliferation or disarmament were not included in the recently concluded Indo-US Strategic dialogue. There is no doubt, however, that, post the Indo-US Civil Nuclear Agreement and the consequent NSG waiver, opportunities for cooperation between India and other countries interested in these issues have increased. Such cooperation was pledged by the Indian Prime Minister at the Washington Nuclear Security Summit in April 2010, and there could be some meaningful cooperation in the context of the CD, for example, in the appointment of a Special Coordinator as proposed by the Indian delegate in 2008, to work on the outlines of a possible mandate for negotiations on nuclear disarmament. At the same time, India has expressed her willingness to participate in the FMCT negotiations in the CD as a state with nuclear weapons and has indicated, though not formally, that her accession to the CTBT would depend on the signature of all other Annex 2 States. The repositioning of India on global nuclear issues has come a long way.

On the other hand, the current nuclear threats to global peace and security were all but ignored by the NPT Review Conference; nuclear terrorism, the dangers of the Pakistani arsenal falling into the hands of unauthorized personnel, the continued existence of the nuclear black market, the dangers of proliferation in the midst of a nuclear renaissance, and States that have been attracting particular attention on nuclear issues. It is true that both the Iran and DPRK issues are with the Security Council and a Review Conference may not be the most appropriate forum for such discussions; however, this points to the inability of the forty year old Treaty to deal with present day problems. Perhaps it is time to think of other forums where these problems could be tackled, for example the IAEA. India's political will to cooperate both in the disarmament debate and in strengthening non-proliferation measures appears to be present; however, such cooperation will have to take place outside the NPT context, given the views of the NPT community on countries like India. There is an obvious need for movement on the part of the NPT community, so that the strengths of countries like India, which are supportive of and able to promote disarmament, at however incremental a pace, can be garnered for a common and collective cause of international peace and security.

THE EUROPEAN UNION & NUCLEAR NON-PROLIFERATION AND DISARMAMENT

Harald Müller

Introduction

The European Union has established itself as a player in the field of nuclear non-proliferation. It has developed a non-proliferation strategy, it has been delivering joint statements to NPT Review Conferences since 1990, it pursues a regulated, common export control policy including the application of sanctions, as presently against Iran, it is involved in crucial negotiations, as, again, in the Iranian case, and it is even accorded a particular task in the 2010 NPT Review Conference's final document (NPT/CONF.2010/L.2, Draft Final Document, 27 May 2010), namely to help prepare a conference of the regional parties in the Middle East to explore ways and means to foster the project of a nuclear weapons free zone: to hold a seminar in advance of this conference in order to facilitate a smooth process and good outcome. All this suggests that the EU is a viable actor in nuclear non-proliferation. This is not trivial. After all, as elaborated in more detail below, the EU has to struggle to find agreement between 27 quite diverse member states. That this succeeds from time to time is no minor achievement. But, by the same token, not all is well. The EU approach has its shortcomings, as was deftly demonstrated by the Irish delegate at the last NPT Review attacking the French representative on the floor on nuclear disarmament. In other words, a more differenciated picture emerges the closer we look at the curious international actor, EU. It is the purpose of this paper to draw such a picture, pointing to failures and achievements, to strengths and weaknesses.

I start with explaining my basic understanding of actors' motivations in international relations as they apply to the field of non-proliferation. I then touch a bit at the EU's institutional structure, and describe the most visible EU proponents in that field and their divergent interests. In the next section, an overview of the development of EU non-proliferation policy since the foundation of the European Community in 1958 follows. Next, the EU Non-proliferation Strategy, adopted in 2003 and since then repeatedly adapted, is analysed. I then take a brief look at three important specific areas of action, the American-Indian nuclear agreement, Iran negotiations, and the recent NPT Review Conference. A brief conclusion points to the strengths and weaknesses of EU non-proliferation policy.

The Framework

Proliferation and Non-Proliferation

Nuclear issues fall broadly into four categories or perspectives: Security, economic welfare, ecological concerns, and morale. Security is involved because of the threat and deterrence potential of nuclear weapons. Economic welfare plays a role because of the potential or actual benefit of nuclear energy and the gains from exporting nuclear facilities, technology, or fuel. Ecological issues are concerned because of the potential of radioactive leaks, major incidents and accidents, and final disposal of spent fuel and other radioactive wastes, but also by nuclear energy's potential contribution, as some see it, to preventing climate change. And morale is implicated by human responsibility for the creation and for human life which is at risk through the enormous devastating potential of both the use of nuclear weapons and major civilian nuclear accidents.

Discussions of proliferation and non-proliferation are frequently narrowed down to a minimum understanding of security embedded in the deterrent value of nuclear weapons. This leads inevitably to the prediction of unstoppable proliferation and even to its endorsement as helpful for world security because it would install plenty of stable deterrence dyads. The prevailing opinion, however, maintans that what is possibly rational from the perspective of the single actor - to have a deterrent against all sorts of threats, and to possess a valuable symbol of international prestige and status - is irrational from the world community's point of view: An increasing number of nuclear armed states would make the probability of a nuclear war, by cold planning and execution, by accidental or unauthorized use, or by unwanted escalation of a crisis, much more likely, and would increase significantly the points of access to weapons and weapons materials to non-state actors. It is for the same reasons that nuclear disarmament is a necessity, as the underlying logic of nuclear proliferation is very simple: "all or none".

I approach state motivations from a common sense rather than an international relations theory point of view: governments, as human beings, are bags of mixed motives in which power, security, greed, and morale appear in different degrees. Some believe in the inherent value of nuclear weapons for their security; others stick to them or strive for them because they believe it makes them great and important. Others renounce them because they think it is unnecessary for their security, because they are covered by security guarantees, or because they would be in danger of becoming a target and thus be less rather than more secure in the end. Finally, some reject them because they find them morally repulsive. In addition, there is the interest to export and to maintain a domestic nuclear industry unmolested by constraints or intrusive inspections, and there is the fear of a radiolocal catastrophe that makes some oppose nuclear power altogether. In analysing non-proliferation policy we have to take into account, first, that motives are mixed, and, second, that the utility of both nuclear weapons and nuclear energy is not objectively given, but is vey much in the eye of the beholder.

The European Union

The EU is a historical miracle and a strange beast. It is a miracle as it brings together countries that have been deadly enemies over centuries in a community where their welfare depends on each other, where they share important aspects of their sovereignty in a supranational setting, and where the thought of war against each other has disappeared as a conceivable possibility. It is as if Pakistan, India, China and Japan would forget the risks of a military conflagration in a common international organisation. For, whatever shortcomings we may hold the EU responsible, this historical achievement is a blessing for the European peoples.

At the same time, the EU is a strange beast: It is no single nation state, but it is also more than just the sum of the members.

It is more than an international organisation, but less than a federation. It has supranational elements, but major activities are conducted in an inter-state mode, and national policies still play an important role. Owing to this complexity, US journalists and most US scholars almost never get the EU perspective right. Since the American and the British media, which look at Europe either sceptically or irrationally hostile, are the main source of world opinion, the outside world gets a quite distorted view of Europe. You read almost always about doom and gloom and the impending decay. Then surprisingly, something happens that rescues the Union from death. The said observers note this surprise in passing and then ride the next wave of doom and gloom. All the while, the EU moves forward from crisis to crisis at a glacier's pace, but each time progressing a bit in its march towards integration.

As a consequence of this complex arrangement, a panoply of actors and action levels influence the European non-proliferation "output". First, there is the important level of nation-state policies. Here, the above dictum of the "different mixed bags" applies. We find staunch defenders of nuclear weapons such as France. We find adherents of extended deterrence, notably among the younger members in the Eastern part of the Union. We find promotors of a stronger move towards arms control and disarmament such as Germany. We find committed, morally driven, non-NATO nuclear weapons abolitionists like Ireland. And we find strong believers in nuclear energy like Slovakia and "reactor abolitionists" such as Austria. The EU nuclear non-proliferation and disarmament policy has to find the common denominator between these widely diverging positions. Like the existence of the EU as a body of peace, the existence of any non-proliferation policy at all would be rated a political miracle.

These policies at the level of the nation-state are not products of a monolithic, linear political process. At the domestic level, they can be heavily contested. In the UK, there exists a lively abolitionist movement with lots of adherents in the Labour and the Liberal parties, and even including part of the military. In Sweden, the idealist disarmament commitment which has ruled Swedish foreign policy for most of the past is contrasted by a pragmatist, US-leaning position at the centre-right, represented by present Foreign Minister Carl Bildt. Germany's former staunch defense of the national nuclear industry has given way to a non-commital stance by the government under the pressure of a strong domestic anti-nuclear movement. Within governments, bureaucracies are struggling with each other: Foreign ministries (with the possible exception of NATO offices in Alliance member states) tend to be more pro-arms control and pro-disarmament, while defense ministries are more conservative. Economic ministries are more inclined to embrace nuclear industries than environmental ministries. The final policies of governmnts are vectors of these various and often mutually opposed forces, influenced, at times, by the personal preferences of top political leaders.

Finally, there exists the Union level. Here, we are right now entering a new phase of interbureaucratic struggles between the Commission which is involved by funding activities in EU non-proliferation policies (whenever the Council enacts a Joint Action) and did not take it with good humour that member states, in the Lisbon Treaty, installed another strong bureaucracy at Council level, including a virtual EU Foreign Minister, Ms. Ashton, and a EU foreign service. The Commission and its President, would have loved to take these functions into their own hands, but failed. Consequenly there is now a guerilla war between these bureaucracies. Its outcome will remain uncertain for some time. Currently, this competition is important at the level of policy implementation rather than of policy-making. The latter realm is in the hands of the member states and their highest organ, the European Council.

A Brief History of EU Non-Proliferation Policy

Before turning to the present shape of this policy, it is appropriate to look as to how we came along to where we are now. The EU – then the European Community – was founded in 1958 with two security concerns in mind, the prevention of the recurrence of three hundred years of permanent fratricide among fellow Europeans, and the quick, common recovery from the remnants of World War II in order to be strong against the Soviet Bloc. Ironically, however, security was banned from the Rome Treaties because France wanted to keep this subject exclusively for her national policy. While a free market for nuclear fuel was created in EURATOM, and external trade was supranationalised, all security-related trade items were excluded from that regulation, as was everything pertaining to nuclear weapons.

Europe made its first steps towards a common foreign policy in the early seventies after Britain's access, but this was still informal coordination devoid of any legal or institutional framework. By practice, a system of working groups at the office director level emerged; when in 1981 such a working group was created for nuclear non-proliferation, this was initially kept secret at French and British insistence. The first public European utterance in this field occurred in 1984, when the Council issued a statement on nuclear exports and the common market for nuclear fuel and technology; this action was forced by the fact that then some, but not all, of the members who belonged to the Nuclear Suppliers Group participants were obliged to observe strict export control rules, while members of EURATOM were not supposed to control mutual nuclear exports to fellow EURATOM members at all.

From this modest beginning, some formulation of non-proliferation policy emerged. The NPT Review Conference of 1985 saw timid EU caucus-sing, while young French diplomats rotated around the meeting rooms and tried to pick up information from their fellow Europeans, as France was not yet a party to the NPT. In 1986, the Single European Act brought the first codification of the common foreign policy (still called "European Political Cooperation") and brought the working group (now: "committees") into the open. In 1990, the European Council issued its first joint declaration on non-proliferation on the eve of the next NPT Review, with France, though still not a party to that Treaty, participating. The European caucus during this conference also had France as a member, since the French took part in the Conference as official observers. All these difficulties were overcome when France joined the NPT in 1992, the same year in which the Europeans also forged a common export control system for nuclear and nuclear related dual-use goods, and adopted the Maastricht Treaty in which Common Foreign and Security Policy (CFSP) became the "Second Pillar" of the Union, and three formal instruments of CFSP, Common Strategy, Joint Action, and Common Position, were introduced to enhance its impact. Nuclear issues were tackled in two committees under the Maastricht Treaty, the Committee on Non-proliferation (CONOP), and the Committee on Disarmament at the United Nations (CODUN). CONOP was the more important body. It was here that the EU prepared its Joint Action for the indefinite extension of the NPT in 1995 which involved an extensive diplomatic campaign with many ambassadorial demarches and high-level visits to the capitals of NPT parties (in order to convince them that indefinite extension was the right thing to do) and of non-parties (in order to persuade them to accede to the NPT). [1]

During the 1995 Review and Extension Conference, the EU coordinated well in the review part which failed in the end, but was not effective, as such, in the extension part which was conducted in a smaller group within a 20-30 delegation, where member states (France, UK, Germany, Sweden) were present in their national capacity, but no EU position was visible. [2] The next review, 2000, was, so far, the high point concerning EU impact on multilateral non-proliferation policy. Well coordinated by the Portugese presidency, the Union prepared a Common Position and managed to insert significant portions of that document into the final declaration. The EU made good use of the fact that its membership, as analysed above, comprises virtually all but the most extreme positions thinkable in the NPT context, and that compromises found within the Union would thus frequently be acceptable as compromises to others. In the decisive small group negotiations on a nuclear disarmament action plan which were held between the P-5 and the New Agenda Coalition, a group of seven disarmament-minded parties from the North and the South (Brazil, Egypt, Ireland, Mexico, New Zealand, South Africa,

---

[1] Harald Müller/Lars van Dassen: From Cacophony to Joint Action: Successes and Shortcomings of European Nuclear Non-Proliferation Policy, in Martin Holland (ed.), Common Foreign and Security Policy. The Record and Reforms, London/Washington, Pinter 1997, S. 52-72

[2] Harald Müller/David Fischer: United Divided. The Europeans and the NPT Extension Conference, PRIF Report 40, Frankfurt 1995

Sweden), EU members were present on either side, and that helped forging a consensus language, although after extended bargaining. In 2003, as a response to the Iraq war and the division this war had left in the Union's ranks, and as a reaction of President George W. Bush's "National Security Strategy" of 2002 that led to raised eyebrows even among the more pro-American members of the EU because of its unfettered unilateralism, the EU adopted first, its own Security Strategy and, as a corollary, a Strategy for the Non-Proliferation of Weapons of Mass Destruction. More substantial analysis will be delivered further below; the important thing was that, the EU had thus agreed on a long-term political framework and guideline for this essential part of CFSP, a framework that was meant to guide both national policies and policies at the Union level. While the document was general enough to accommodate the preferences of all members, it left room enough for members desiring to do so to go beyond some of the principles and envisaged actions (e.g. on disarmament for the more pacifist members). But there was the obligation under the Maastricht and Amsterdam (the successor treaty to Maastricht) Treaties not to act counter to the letter and the spirit of the two strategies. In the office of the Special Representative for CFSP, a position established in the Amsterdam Treaty, a department on non-proliferation was installed, headed by a Special Representative for Non-proliferation to supervise the implementation of the Non-proliferation Strategy. This department has been issuing annual reports on the Strategy's implementation ever since.

The 2005 Review Conference saw a badly split Union, even though it had been possible to agree on a Common Position briefly before the event. France, together with the US, declared that the 2000 Final Declaration with its agreed language on disarmament was not anymore valid, very much to the chagrin of the two EU-NAC members, Ireland and Sweden, and the bulk of the other EU non-nuclear weapon states. A procedural play of mutual blockage, which prevented the Conference from adopting an agenda for almost three weeks, was played by the US and Egypt as the antagonists. It was the EU that breached the deadlock in the end, but it did not help to produce a successful out come of the Review in 2005.[3]

EU Non-proliferation Strategy: An Overview[4]

The European strategy, adopted in 2003, is coded in the following four documents:

- The outline of an EU security strategy, which was compiled with the High Representative for foreign policy in charge,[5]

- The statement of the European Council on the proliferation of weapons of mass destruction (WMD),[6]

---

[3] Har ald Müller: A T reaty in T roubled W aters. R eflections on the F ailed NPT Review Conference, in: International Spectator , 40(3) 2005, 33-44

[4] F or the f ollowing, cf. Nuklear e Krisen und tr ansatlantischer Dissens. Amerikanische und europäische Antworten auf aktuelle Probleme der Weiterverbreitung v on K ernwaffen, Fr ankfurt/M, HSFK-Report 9/2003

[5] "A Secure Europe in a Better World. Draft European Security Strategy Presented by the EU High R epresentative for the Common F oreign and S ecurity Policy, Javier Solana, to the European Council," June 20, 2003 in Thessaloniki, Greece (http://www.dgap.org/english/ tip/tip0303/solana200603.htm, July 28, 2003).

[6] "EU Presidency Conclusions," Thessaloniki, June 19-20, 2003, Annex II (htp:/ /www.acronym.org.uk/docs/0306/doc13.htm, July 28, 2003).

- The principles for an EU strategy against the proliferation of WMD,[7] and

- An action plan for the completion and practical application of these principles.[8]

The threat analysis in the Security Strategy which informs the approach to non-proliferation describes the proliferation of WMD, terrorism, and the combination of both as the most dangerous risks. It links these factors to the poverty problem as well as regional conflicts. The Europeans handle the proliferation issue without a moral devaluation of the states, which are under the suspicion of attempting to acquire weapons of mass destruction. The reason is that the Europeans want to maintain the possibility of the "stretched out hands". In the EU security strategy, the UN plays a central role as a factor of global security order, and thereby, in the field of WMD. For the Europeans, the various non-proliferation regimes are the most important factor and they would like to see them being strengthened further.

Democratization, in which the Europeans believe in deeply, should be realized by development aid, trade agreements, and conditionality. There is no direct relation to the proliferation problem. Export controls represent an important instrument. Eventually, when no other strategy is effective, even Europe, for

---

[7] "Basic Principles for an EU Strategy against Proliferation of Weapons of Mass Destruction, EU Presidency Conclusions," Thessaloniki, June 19-20, 2003, pts. 99/100 (http://www.acronym.org.uk/docs/0306/doc13.htm, July 28, 2003).

[8] "Action Plan for the Implementatioon of the Basic Principles for an EU Strategy against Proliferation of Weapons of Mass Destruction, EU Presidency Conclusions," Thessaloniki, June 19-20, 2003, pts. 99/100 (http://www.acronym.org.uk/docs/0306/doc13.htm, July 28, 2003).

the first time, declared now to be willing to consider the use of military operations to enforce non-proliferation. In the EU-"action plan", nineteen of twenty-two steps are designed to strengthen or implement international regimes as well as diplomatic activities or bilateral aid. The aspect of military operations is only mentioned in step 13, where the EU commits itself to work towards a resolution of the Security Council, which defines the proliferation of weapons of mass destruction as a threat to peace and international security. That step would open the door to sanctions according to Chapter VII of the UN Charter. Apart from that, the document deals with the strengthening of the *capacities* of the EU for handling the weapons of mass destruction problem.

As regards possible military operations for the purpose of enforcing non-proliferation, the European document refers to Chapter VII of the UN Charter – economic and military sanctions to be imposed by the Security Council – and defines the Security Council as the "last arbiter of non-proliferation" – as intended in the multilateral regimes.[9] The Europeans associate *pre-emption* with the legal decision process of international law. That is logical in so far as the non-proliferation regimes have established legal systems themselves for weapons of mass destruction, including the NPT for whose protection the international community, through the UNSC, can use legitimate force in the most extreme of cases. That has always been implicitly contained in the fact that, according to Art. 12 of the IAEA Statute, the UNSC is the arbiter in cases when the IAEA finds that a state is not in compliance with its safeguards obligations and cannot grant that the nuclear program of that state is serving exclusively peaceful

---

9   See Basic Principles, §§4, 6.

purposes. In cases where such a state of affairs would be assessed as a threat to peace and international security, the UNSC is authorized to mandate the entire range of instruments stated in Chapter VII, including military operations.

The Europeans do not identify non-democratic regimes with proliferation threats. Rather, they rely on coexistence, hoping that a political evolution will take place in the states of concern.[10] Regime change is not the predominant strategy for non-proliferation. For that reason, the EU attaches great importance to the strengthening and development of the international regimes. After all, the purpose of these regimes is to make security cooperation policy possible even though the cooperating parties come from different political systems.

The last update occured in 2008;[11] the wide range of actions envisaged included, *inter alia*, staff training for non-proliferation officials, a survey and identification of best practices in the transfer control of intangible technology, a commitment to contribute up to 25 million EURO to the planned IAEA fuel bank; a joint proliferation threat assessment; the creation of a European network of think-tanks concerned with proliferation issues; setting up procedures for the punishment of proliferation financing; wide range measures supported by EU money to make fissile material and radioactive sources in more than fourty countries more secure; conducting non-proliferation dialogues with Egypt, the Persian

---

[10] See, e.g., "A Secure Europe in a Better World", p. 6.

[11] Council of the European Union, New lines for action by the EU in combating the proliferation of weapons of mass destruction and their delivery systems, Brussels, Dec. 8, 2008

Gulf states, and ASEAN.[12] This selection gives an impression of the scope of activities which the EU, in addition to the individual policies of member states, is conducting in this field.

The American-Indian Deal, Iran, the 2010 NPT Review Conference

The US-Indian Deal

Europe had been, till the end of the eighties, the site of resistance to the American-Canadian drive to move export policies towards "full scope safeguards", the requirement that all nuclear activities in a recipient country should be under IAEA comprehensive safeguards before export licenses for nuclear or nuclear-related dual use transfers could be granted. It was with Germany's shifting of sides on this issue in 1990 that "full scope safeguards" became the standard for export licensing in the NPT community, as well as in the Nuclear Suppliers Group. The "Principles and Objectives" adopted by the NPT Review Conference in 1995, together with the extension resolution, and similar language endorsed by the final declaration of the 2000 Review Conference sealed this requirement as politically binding NPT policy.

When the Bush Administration negotiated a nuclear cooperation agreement with India that would free transfers to India from this requirement, the EU was even further advanced in its export policy: All members had "Additional Protocols" in force and were prepared to make not only comprehensive

---

[12] Council of the European Union, Six-monthly Progress Report on the implementation of the EU Strategy against the Proliferation of Weapons of Mass Destruction (2010/I) as endorsed by the Council on 14 June 2010

safegaurds, but also the application of Additional Protocols in the recipient countries the requirement for any form of transfer.

The US-Indian deal shattered this unity. EU members took quite different stances on it. The UK, as ever, supported what the Americans had done no matter what; possibly, Commonwealth empathy played also a role. France returned to its old empathy for India. One should not forget that the French Atomic Energy Commission had sent a telegram of congratulation after India's very first nuclear explosive test in 1974. While France had followed Germany in adopting full scope safeguards as a pre-condition of nuclear transfers, the Indian civilian nuclear market looked always very attractive to Paris; the US-Indian deal meant for the French nuclear industry the liberation from the NSG/NPT nuclear export straight jacket. Paris was thus in no mood to oppose it. On the other side of the aisle there were countries like Austria, Sweden or Ireland that were opposed to the deal as a matter of principle. In the middle stood Germany, where there was a strong mood against the agreement in Parliament because of its unsatisfactory disarmament stipulations, but where the government – reluctantly – came to the conclusion that opposing it would hurt German interests more, and grudgingly went along.

When the decisive session of the NSG took place, the Europeans were, not unexpectedly, divided. Some of the more disarmament and non-proliferation committed smaller members held out in opposition very long. But lacking any support, and suffering some pressures, from the larger powers, they did not feel strong enough to cast a veto (which, under the rules of procedure of the NSG, would have been possible in principle). The EU as such (represented by the EU Commission in the NSG) kept silent and let the member states take positions. In one of the most defining practical issues of the day in the field of non-proliferation and disarmament.[13]

The EU and diplomacy on the Iranian issue

European non-proliferation diplomacy towards Iran started earnestly after the September 2003 Resolution of the IAEA Board of Governors, which determined that Iran had not complied for some years with its undertakings contained in the safeguards agreement pursuant to the NPT and was showing insufficient cooperation to clarify all outstanding issues. The Europeans began talks with Iran, which were characterized by a temporary success. During a visit of the foreign ministers of Germany, France and Great Britain, Tehran promised the "suspension" of its enrichment program, joining the Additional Protocol, and making its entire nuclear program transparent for the IAEA. The Europeans recognized the legitimacy of the Iranian civil nuclear program and promised technical support.

Typically, this start was characterized by the initiative of the major member states and by-passed in the first round the EU institutions. This was remedied shortly later, after other members had expressed their concern about this triadic outbreak from the EU CFSP. Afterwards, the EU Representative, Javier Solana, was fully involved, making frequent trips to Iran on his own. What had emerged in the first round: EU offers - Iranian seeming acceptance, delay, insufficient implementation, then next round and so on - developed as a regular pattern, notably after the radical wing of the Iranian political elite took over with the election of

---

[13] Christos Katsioulis/Christian Mölling, NPT Review 2020. What Role for the EU? Berlin, Friedrich Ebert Stiftung 2010, p. 7

President Ahmadinedjad in 2005. Nevertheless, the Europeans tried their best to keep the negotiations alive, succeeding in the end even to secure high-level participation by the USA in the last phase of the Bush Administration.[14] When all diplomatic offers – notably the much more cooperative attitude towards Iran by President Obama – did not bear fruit and Iran used sophisticated "salami tactics" to creep closer and closer towards the nuclear option, the Europeans entered a more confrontational mood, concluding that a rapproachment with Iran on friendly terms was probably impossible. The consequence was their support for sharper UN sanctions and, eventually, agreeing on additional sanctions imposed by the EU in parallel to the United States. Throughout the process, EU positions were found after intense and controversial debates. Among the three big EU member states, Germany, with the best traditional relations to Iran, was most cooperatively minded, while France (under President Sarkozy) took a much more confrontational position. In the broader membership, countries with good relations with the developing world, like Sweden argued against turning the sanctions srew. It bespeaks the devastating impression of President Ahmadinedjad's policies that eventually all would agree that more determined sanctions could not be avoided.

The focus on the Iranian issue can be concluded from the fact that between 2007 and now, no less than eight different decisions by the Council of the European Union were taken.[15]

---

[14] Tom Sauer, Struggling on the W orld Scene: An o ver-ambitious EU v ersus a committed Ir an, in: European S ecurity, 17 (2) 2008, 273-293; Sebastian Harnisch, Minilateral Cooperation and Transatlantic Coalition-Buidling: The E3/EU-3 Iran Initiative, in: Eur opean Security 16 (1), 2007 , 1-27

[15] http://www.consilium.europa.eu/showPage.aspx?id=718&lang=en

The EU at the 2010 NPT Review Conference

The EU showed a limited profile at this conference. The EU "foreign minister" Ashton spoke for the EU in the general debate instead of the Presidency as in the past. The Ashton statement relied on the Common Position which the EU had finalised little more than a month before the Conference.[16] The Spanish Presidency coordinated the EU caucus during the REVCON. Consequently there was more written EU input into the Conference proceedings than in previous Review Conferences. The Common Position was introduced as a working paper and utilized as basis for contributions by the EU to the deliberations of the Main Committees and the subsidiary bodies. The EU introduced working papers on crucial issues, such as the Middle East, IAEA verification, withdrawal from the Treaty, and the verification system of CTBT. During the negotiation phase, the EU proposed text passage from these statements as language for the Committee reports and, in the end game, for the final declaration.

Despite this considerable input, the EU left a rather subdued impression for four reasons. First, the Common Position expressed no more than the least common denominator. On nuclear disarmament, this common ground was not very substantial, at least as new initiatives were concerned. This was due to the attitude of France in particular. The French delegation did not accept any concessions regarding France's national positions. Even on substrategic weapons on which the EU Common Position

---

[16] COUNCIL DECISION 2010/212/CFSP, of 29 March 2010 relating to the position of the European Union for the 2010 Review Conference of the Parties to the Treaty on the Non-Pr oliferation of Nuclear W eapons

contained Germany-inspired text, France and Great Britain kept silent on the floor without any supportive statements. With this disarmament minimalism, the EU was not very impressive.

Second, the Spanish Presidency restricted itself to presenting the respective EU positions or simply announced that the EU would submit language to the chair for his consideration. The EU did not enter debate or react to the contributions of other delegations. In negotiations, however, only engaging in debate earns you a profile – this is not what the EU did. Third, almost all EU members kept Union discipline. Delegations left the floor to the Presidency and took the floor at best to support what Spain had said. Only Ireland, Italy, the Netherlands and Germany entered the debate sporadically. Fourth, France was the one country to deviate from EU discipline by speaking frequently and extensively. While paying formally their due to the EU, the French then pursued national positions which went considerably beyond what EU had agreed upon, notably on disarmament and non-proliferation. These interventions exposed often an arrogant and provocative tone which was resented by the NAM. France wanted to be applauded for her past disarmament achievements while simultaneously rejecting any more disarmament commitments at present.

Because the EU Presidency and the membership remained mute while France was speaking time and again, the undesirable impression emerged that France spoke for the EU. The EU did not become any more popular this way; reportedly, it did good work in the end-game when the small-group negotiatiated, but only 14 other delegations, including three from the EU, participated there and the course of the talks was kept confidential: When the EU star shined, only few were watching.

Conclusion

The EU is a hybrid association of states. It is not a hierarchy with a decision-making center like a nation state. As long as this is the case, and this might be quite long, it makes little sense for beating up the EU for not "speaking with one voice". The EU *cannot* speak with one voice all times in all places and on all issues: It is just not in the nature of the beast it is. It is miraculous enough that the EU *does* speak with one voice on many issues frequently and in significant places. This is what we can expect; we can also expect the EU to make slow progress to enhance the number of issues, times and places as well as the operative detail of commonality. But progress is necessarily slow, and it is the direction of more commonality, not high speed, which is the appropriate standard against which we can measure the Union's achievements.

This applies to all fields of policy, to all areas of Common Foreign and Security Policy, and to non-proliferation policy in particular. That there is such a policy against all odds of the internal divisions, just by the different status of the states and the ensuing preferences is respectable. That this policy frequently takes place only on the lowest common denominator is inevitable in the light of the diversity of attitudes, convictions, and interests of the member states.

On the other hand, this same diversity does not always amount to a political weakness; at times it is a strength. For example, the EU is capable of pursuing impressive and powerful diplomatic campaigns by mobilising the complete diplomatic efforts of all members. Likewise, the EU can exploit – and has exploited at times – the fact that contending interests place members in opposed groups: These members can work in their respective group for building bridges, as it happened during the 2000 NPT Review.

In the last ten years, a focussed central bureaucracy has emerged in Brussels which supports the members' efforts, acts at times in their name and, at other times, takes initiatives for persuading the members to pursue certain activities. The possibility to fund actions through member states' contribution, through the Commission budget, through means available to the Council Secretariat or through all, gives more flexibility than is available to individual nation states.

In adition, the particular relations of individual members to other actors (France to the Francophony, Sweden to a variety of non-aligned states, Germany to Russia, to give only a few examples) or the willingness of leading EU states to take initiatives (as in the case of Iran in 2003) opens additional opportunities for the EU to have an international impact, provided such unilateral impulses are transformed into common action by all.

EU procedures are time-consuming, hierarchical action in a nation-state like manner is not in the cards. Quick reaction in crises is thus no EU strength. It is further impeded by the inclination and practice of the two permanent members of the UNSC to celebrate this privileged position by pursuing national positions most of the time, offering at best minimum coordination with the EU membership (to which they are in principle obliged since the Maastricht Treaty).

In political issues where the interests of EU member states diverge strongly, or where the national interests of some confront the moral convictions of others, as on nuclear disarmament or on the peaceful uses of nuclear energy, the lowest common denominator to be achieved is very low indeed. Common positions, even if the members manage to agree on one in the end, are then vague and not very relevant.

There is no doubt that, presently, the immobility of the French position on disarmament issues, and the tenacious insistence that being a nuclear weapon state is part and parcel of French identity is a major brake on quicker progress in EU non-proliferation and disarmament policy. But times are changing as they have in the past, and a new generation of French politicians and diplomats might see things more flexibly than the present one. Until such time, the EU will at least be able to address proliferation crises, support moderate steps forward in disarmament, and consider, propose and support measures to strengthen the non-proliferation toolbox. This is not the optimum; but looking back to where the Union started from, it is still a lot.

NUCLEAR WEAPONS STATES OUTSIDE THE NPT AND DISARMAMENT: TRENDS AND RESPONSES

Brig. Gurmeet Kanwal (Retd.) and Dr. Monika Chansoria

Introduction

At the end of the five-yearly review of the Nuclear Non-Proliferation Treaty (NPT) in May 2010, 189 members of the NPT once again extended their support to the moribund treaty. They reaffirmed their commitment to the NPT's basic goals: nuclear disarmament, non-proliferation and the promotion of the use of nuclear power for peaceful purposes only. Even Iran joined in although with enthusiasm that had been put on to avoid being labelled a treaty wrecker and, simultaneously, worked towards blocking moves for tougher rules to be introduced. Even as the NPT review conference was giving final touches to a contentious resolution, the United Nations (UN) Security Council was discussing tough new sanctions to be imposed on Iran for violating NPT obligations and consistently denying access to key nuclear facilities to IAEA inspectors.

Since the last review in 2005 that had ended in a controversial stalemate after the NPT had been extended in perpetuity earlier, India, Israel and Pakistan have remained outside the treaty and North Korea has walked out of the treaty and tested nuclear warheads on at least two occasions. During the review conference Egypt upbraided Israel for not paying heed to the cherished desire of its neighbours to promote the West Asia as a nuclear free zone. Emboldened by Iran's defiance, Syria too has been refusing to allow international inspectors to visit the site of its secret nuclear reactor that was destroyed by Israeli warplanes in 2007. In short, while there has been no large-scale move to acquire nuclear weapons, the record of the NPT has been a mixed bag of both, success and failure.

Back in 1946, when the UN General Assembly had affirmed its determination to eliminate the production of "atomic weapons" and other weapons of mass destruction (WMD), the implementation of the proposal was plagued by several major impediments including monitoring and enforcement. Further, the confabulations at the Conference on Disarmament (CD) in Geneva have been viewed with much significance given that it is the sole multilateral international forum for deliberations on issues pertaining to global disarmament. In spite of serious efforts towards achieving unexceptionable international goals, the CD has been unable to adopt an agenda for almost a decade, leading to the stagnation of the global process of arms control and disarmament.

The changing political climate of the post-Cold War period prompted in-depth analysis of the UN's role in advancing regional approaches to disarmament in the conventional field. The added value of a regional approach to UN disarmament efforts has been acknowledged for more than three decades, finally leading to the adoption of guidelines and recommendations for regional approaches to disarmament by the UN Disarmament Commission (UNDC) in 1993. The UNDC concluded that regional and global approaches to disarmament and arms limitation complemented each other and should be pursued simultaneously, in order to promote regional and international peace and security.

The ongoing regional approaches to disarmament within the framework of the various Security Council and General Assembly mandates also underscore the debate surrounding nations which have pronounced themselves as nuclear weapon states (NWS) outside the realm of the Nuclear Non-proliferation Treaty be it in South Asia (India and Pakistan), West Asia (Israel) or Northeast Asia (North Korea), as also states like Iran which are signatories but appear to have ambitions to acquire nuclear weapons.

Disarmament: A Grand Bargain?

The argument for nuclear disarmament, more specifically the US's unilateral disarmament was put forth by none other than Paul Nitze, who acquired the image of a hawk as far as shaping American nuclear policy during the Cold War years was concerned. Suggesting disarmament as an imperative to security, Nitze asserted, "I see no compelling reason why we should not unilaterally get rid of our nuclear weapons... To maintain them is costly and adds nothing to our security... In view of the fact that we can achieve our objectives with conventional weapons, there is nothing to be gained through the use of our nuclear arsenal."[1] Taking this argument further George Perkovich commented on the ever-growing proliferation threat and stated:[2]

> So long as some states are allowed to possess nuclear weapons legitimately and derive the benefits that flow from them, then other states in the system will want them too... The proliferation threat thus stems from the existence and possession of nuclear weapons and theft-prone materials, not merely from the intentions of today's 'axis of evil'.

There has been much deliberation regarding President Barack Obama's speech delivered at Prague in April 2009—peddled as a commitment towards achieving nuclear disarmament. Nevertheless, it would not be prudent to read too much into the speech which was high on rhetoric since related US policies and actions thereafter signal different intentions altogether. As part of a conceptual discourse, Obama spoke about "the role of nuclear weapons in our national security strategy," without any elucidation of how to get rid of them. While he laid emphasis on disarmament, the White House on the contrary, simultaneously went on to request one of the larger increases in warhead spending history. In the eventuality of this request being realised, US warhead spending would rise by nearly 10 per cent in a single year. Obama's assertion towards disarmament came with a rider, "... in the meantime, the United States will maintain a safe, secure and effective arsenal to deter any adversary." Even prior to assuming

---

[1] Paul Nitze, "A Threat Mostly to Ourselves," *The New York Times*, October 28, 1999.

[2] For more details see, George Perkovich, "Bush's Nuclear Revolution: A Regime Change in Nonproliferation," *Foreign Affairs*, vol. 82, no. 2, March/April 2003.

office as President of the United States, President-elect Obama had made a statement acknowledging, "… as long as nuclear weapons exist, we'll retain a strong deterrent."[3] Therefore, not surprisingly, Los Alamos National Laboratory, the biggest target of the Obama largesse, would see a 22 per cent budget increase—the largest since 1944. In particular, funding for a new plutonium 'pit' factory complex over there would more than double, signaling a commitment to produce new nuclear weapons a decade hence.[4] The FY 2011 budget requisitions reflect the concept of extended deterrence for which investments are all likely to continue.

This US defence budget projects spending requests to go up to approximately $700 billion without any existing programmes being stalled. The budget request includes a staggering $600 million increase for the nuclear weapons programme to a total of about $7 billion—thus leading to a question mark over whether Obama's vision on disarmament promulgated in Prague would correspond to this upswing in the US defence budgeting.

It would be pertinent to mention here that while many US administrations have discussed the issue of disarmament, none have actually moved towards any tangible solutions for achieving this goal. Secretary of State Madeline Albright spoke earlier of "… our NPT commitment to move toward the elimination of nuclear weapons… is a worthy goal, embraced by Presidents of both parties, including President Clinton."[5] What could be interpreted as the most telling policy statement on disarmament

[3] Speech by President-elect Barack Obama, Summit on Confronting New Threats, West Lafayette, (Indiana) July 16, 2008.

[4] Greg Melb, "The Obama Disarmament Paradox," *Bulletin of the Atomic Scientists* February 4, 2010.

was a comment by former spokesperson of the US Department of State, Nicholas Burns. When he was questioned regarding US plans to keep nuclear weapons indefinitely while advocating the long-term goals of elimination, Burns replied in the affirmative vis-à-vis keeping the US nuclear arsenal and stressed that the US continued to believe that nuclear deterrence played a key role in defending the vital national security interests of the US. Although Burns affirmed that elimination was a goal that successive US administrations had committed themselves to, he urged that we must live in the real world while preparing practically for the security of the US. Interestingly, this sentiment can be traced back to the early 1980s when a Harvard Nuclear Study Group comprising Samuel P Huntington, Joseph S Nye Jr., Albert Carnesale, Paul Doty, Stanley Hoffmann, Scott D Sagan and Derek Bok arrived at similar findings and proclaimed, "The singular hope of survival came along living alongside nuclear weapons."[6]

NPT Compliance

At the 2010 NPT Review Conference in May 2010, a number of key issues including universality of the Treaty, nuclear disarmament, nuclear non-proliferation, promotion and strengthening of safeguards; measures to advance the peaceful use of nuclear energy, safety and security and measures to address withdrawal from the Treaty, were taken up for deliberation.

---

[5] Speech by US Secretary of State, Madeleine Albright, Henry L Stimson Center, Washington, D.C., June 10, 1998.

[6] For more details on the study see, *Living with Nuclear Weapons*, A Harvard Nuclear Study Group comprising Albert Carnesale, Samuel P Huntington, Joseph S Nye Jr., Paul Doty, Stanley Hof fmann, S cott D. Sagan and Der ek Bok, (Cambridge: Harvard University Press, 1983).

Adding to all these probable measures being undertaken, UN Secretary General, Ban Ki-moon stated that reviewing implementation of the NPT would further advance the goal of full nuclear disarmament. By virtue of being the only binding commitment in a multilateral treaty, the NPT represents the commitment of the NWS towards disarmament. However, the bifurcation of states into nuclear '*haves*' and '*have-nots*' has often triggered disparate views regarding many facets of NPT's implementation. As far as compliance is concerned, there could be focus on whether the NWS are complying with Article IV (Technical Cooperation) and Article VI (Nuclear Disarmament) of the Treaty. On the other hand, attention could well be on the non-nuclear weapon states (NNWS) and their compliance with Article II (Obligation not to develop or receive nuclear weapons) and Article III (Safeguards).

Although Article VI is indistinctly worded, the NPT's disarmament pledge was given more lethality in the "Principles and Objectives on Nuclear Non-Proliferation and Disarmament" whose adoption in 1995 was an integral part of the collective decision to extend the NPT indefinitely, and in the even stronger commitment made in the Final Document agreed upon at the 2000 NPT Review Conference.[7] Under Article VI of the treaty, the NPT signatories including the NWS states had promised to, "pursue negotiations in good faith" for the "cessation of the nuclear arms race at an early date; to nuclear disarmament; and on a treaty on general and complete disarmament under strict and effective international control." The NNWS would have never agreed to

---

[7] 2000 Review Conference of the Parties to the Treaty on the Non-Proliferation of Nuclear Weapons, Final Document, vol. 1, New York, 2000, p. 14.

abstain from acquiring nuclear weapons without this pledge.[8] It was way back in 1967, that US negotiators had argued, "it would not be feasible to incorporate specific obligations [toward disarmament] in the treaty itself. The differences that have prevented agreement on these measures have not yet been resolved."[9] Although the 1995 and 2000 NPT Review Conferences identified 'practical' steps toward disarmament, disagreements about the legal status of those steps and their implications for non-compliance still persist.[10]

Perhaps the gravest challenge to the NPT is the looming threat of non-compliance by signatories. Subsequently, the onus now appears to have shifted to close any loopholes allowing states to produce nuclear materials that could be used to pursue a nuclear weapons programme for military purposes under the guise of a civilian nuclear programme. A potential instrument for this was a new model for safeguards namely the Additional Protocol (1997). States running enrichment or reprocessing facilities could readily produce fissile materials for weapons—clandestinely and/or after withdrawing from the NPT (a classic case study being that of North Korea during the decade of the 1990s). However, it should be clear to the NWS that the intransigence of the

---

[8] Tom Sauer, "Nuclear Proliferation and Nuclear Disarmament: Two Sides of the Same Coin," Institute for International and Eur opean Policy, Working Paper no. 17, May 2005, p. 7.

[9] For more details see, Mason Wi llrich, *Non-Proliferation Treaty: Framework for Nuclear Arms Control*, (Virginia:The Michie Company, 1969), p. 100.

[10] Darryl Howlett, John Simpson, Har ald Mueller and Bruno Tertrais, "Effective Non-Proliferation:The European Union and the 2005 NPT Review Conference,"*Chaillot Paper*, no. 77, April 2005, Institute for Security Studies, European Union, Paris, p. 13.

major weapon states in relation to their own nuclear arsenals strengthens the hands of pro-nuclear weapon factions in threshold states (especially Iran), thereby providing an additional push toward proliferation.[11] Citing the case of the debate surrounding the Iranian nuclear pursuit in this context, Ashton Carter has stated, "The decisions of in-between states are probably strongly shaped by their perception of the nuclear 'order' that the United States represents and leads, partly by example."[12]

Therefore, if comprehensive global disarmament were to eventually come true then the most imperative query would be relating to states attempting to cross the nuclear threshold such as Iran, given its relentless efforts at achieving nuclear knowhow which it claims is exclusively for 'civilian purposes.' In such a scenario, it seems exceedingly unlikely that NWS, most significantly, the US, shall do away with their existing stockpiles of nuclear weapons. While NWS within the NPT shall continue to remain skeptical as far as completely eliminating their nuclear stockpiles, the ones outside the realm of the NPT (India, Pakistan and Israel) are bound to be even more recalcitrant. A rational explanation for this wariness could be the strategic advantage that the big powers, especially the US, might gain given their ability to exert influence globally. Further, as William Walker has argued, many US allies feel constrained by the possession of nuclear weapons by states that would otherwise have only a slight leverage in international affairs—North Korea is a prime example.

---

[11] John Holdr en, "Nuclear Nonpr oliferation and US r esponsibilities," *Chicago Tribune*, June 2, 1998; also see S cott Sagan, "Wh y Do States B uild Nuclear Weapons?" *International Security*, Winter 1996/1997 , p. 73.

[12] Ashton Carter , "How to Counter WMD ," *Foreign Af fairs*, vol.83, no. 5, September/October 2004.

States with Nuclear Weapons (SNW) outside the NPT fold

India

Since its independence, India has faced many external threats and challenges, including the disadvantage of living in a dangerous nuclear neighbourhood. Following the India-China border war in 1962, Beijing declared itself a NWS in 1964. The Sino-Pak WMD axis, by means of which Islamabad acquired nuclear weapons capability in 1986-87 with covert help from China is well known. Following the Pokhran tests in May 1998, India declared itself a state with nuclear weapons. New Delhi's nuclear arsenal should not be interpreted as anything other than a political weapon that is meant only to deter the use and threat of use of nuclear weapons against India. India has abjured the use of tactical/theatre nuclear weapons.

India faces a paradoxical situation: nuclear weapons are critically important for national security because of the threats and challenges stemming from long-standing territorial and boundary disputes with China and Pakistan, but nuclear weapons are inherently destabilising in nature. India's nuclear doctrine centres on a 'no first use' policy with 'credible minimum deterrence.' In the interest of strategic stability, India is willing to absorb a 'first strike' and has declared its intention of launching 'massive punitive retaliation' to cause unacceptable damage to the adversary. Consequently, India follows a 'counter value' targeting strategy. India practices strategic restraint and believes in entering into nuclear confidence building and risk reduction measures. It is in India's interest to ensure that political and military crises in Southern Asia are not allowed to degenerate uncontrollably into the breakdown of nuclear deterrence. The Indian leadership is acutely conscious of its responsibility to ensure strategic stability. It is aware that a state armed with nuclear weapons must contribute positively to deterrence stability through a high state of operational readiness of its nuclear arsenal combined with pragmatic nuclear diplomacy, including arms control and non-proliferation policies.

Nuclear Disarmament. Despite not having signed the NPT and the Comprehensive Test Ban Treaty (CTBT), India has been in compliance with all the provisions of these key treaties. Nonetheless, India has persistently been opposed to the NPT since the late 1960s. India's consistent view has been that the NPT is an inequitable instrument dividing the world into nuclear *'haves'* and *'have nots.'* India has advocated that the key to resolving the global predicament of nuclear proliferation lies in comprehensive nuclear disarmament of which New Delhi has been a strong advocate. While deliberating over the CTBT negotiations during the early 1990s, India had argued that the CTBT had wandered away from its original objective of serving as a primary instrument of controlling the nuclear arms race. Rather, it was perceived as turning into an instrument of non-proliferation seeking to impose an embargo upon nations which were on the nuclear learning curve. India's long-standing commitment to nuclear disarmament is reflected in its voluntary renunciation of any further nuclear testing and an untarnished non-proliferation record among the NWS.

On June 9, 1988, Prime Minister Rajiv Gandhi presented to the UN General Assembly a time bound action plan for total nuclear disarmament, which later became known as the Rajiv Gandhi Action Plan.[13] A decade later, while delivering a statement in Parliament on December 15, 1998, Prime Minister, Atal Behari Vajpayee spelt out the principal elements of India's nuclear policy.[14] Amongst the significant aspects of the speech were, "India's resolve to preserve its nuclear independence, minimum nuclear deterrence, no first use, non-use of nuclear weapons against non-nuclear powers, and a firm commitment to the elimination of nuclear weapons." Prime Minister Vajpayee re-stated India's readiness to work towards the successful conclusion of the Fissile Material Cut-off Treaty (FMCT). Further, while participating in discussions at the CD on an FMCT in 2007, New Delhi stated that it would not pose a hurdle toward any movement on drafting an FMCT as long as it is 'universal, non-discriminatory, and internationally and effectively verifiable.'

It would be pertinent to mention here that it was at the Non-Aligned Summit in Durban in 1998, that the Movement accepted India's proposal for an international conference to arrive at an agreement on a phased programme for the complete elimination of all nuclear weapons. Subsequently, at the Millennium Summit of the UN in September 2000, the Indian Prime Minister asserted that India's policy is based on "responsibility and restraint" and that India would continue to press for universal, verifiable nuclear disarmament with undiminished commitment, even while safeguarding "our strategic

---

[13] "A World Free of Nuclear Weapons", Prime Minister Rajiv Gandhi at the United Nations Gener al Assembly , New Y ork, June 9, 1988 http://www.indianembassy.org/policy/Disarmament/disarm15.htm

[14] Rahul Bedi, "India Confirms Nuclear Policy," *Jane's Defence Weekly*, December 23, 1998.

space and autonomy in decision-making. International peace cannot be divorced from the need for equal and legitimate security for all."[15] One of the distinguishing features of India's nuclear doctrine proposed by the National Security Advisory Board in August 1999 was that it was "... anchored in India's continued commitment to global, verifiable and non-discriminating nuclear disarmament..."[16] also described as one of India's key national security objectives. Considering the use of nuclear weapons as the most critical threat to humanity and to peace and stability in the international system, the doctrine paper clearly pointed out India's desire to see the world completely rid of nuclear weapons.

It could be argued that owing to the vested interests of the five original NWS in a relentless pursuit to safeguard their own nuclear weapon stocks for the foreseeable future, progress towards total nuclear disarmament has been frustratingly slow. In February 2000, while addressing the UN Advisory Board on Disarmament, Secretary General, Kofi Annan chided the NWS for their lack of commitment to nuclear disarmament and warned of a dangerous new arms race looming large on the horizon. Annan stated, "If we are to even dream of a world free of nuclear weapons by the end of the 21st century, we should start taking new and effective measures for nuclear disarmament and non-proliferation right now."[17] However, such calls continue to go unheeded and there is little urgency in the deliberations within the CD at Geneva.

---

[15] Address by Atal Behari Vajpayee, Prime Minister of India, Millennium Summit of the United Nations, as cited in, *Strategic Digest*, vol. XXX, no. 10, New Delhi, October 2000, pp. 1431-1435.

[16] Ibid.

[17] Cited in, " Annan for Effective N-Disarmament Measure s", *Hindustan Times*, February 4, 2000.

The only good news is that a more intense debate is shaping up vis-à-vis why nuclear weapons should not be eliminated from the face of the earth.[18] If this major initiative were to bear fruit, India would benefit immensely since total or universal nuclear disarmament would change the strategic equation in South Asia in India's favour arising from conventional weapons superiority and make India an economic and military superpower to reckon with.

In an address to the Indian Parliament on August 13, 2007, Prime Minister, Manmohan Singh reiterated "… India's long-standing commitment to the noble ideas of nuclear disarmament and refusal to participate in any arms race, including a nuclear arms race… Our commitment to universal, non-discriminatory and total elimination of nuclear weapons remains undiminished."[19] The leading defence analyst K Subrahmanyam, also avers "… the route to elimination of nuclear weapons is through de-legitimisation and it starts with 'no-first use'."[20] As a corollary, India is willing to absorb a 'first strike' and has declared its intention of launching massive punitive retaliation to cause unacceptable damage to the adversary. In sum, India stands alone

---

[18] Andrew J. Goodpaster and Howard Berman have stated, "In our view, nuclear weapons are of declining political and military utility in both addressing the residual threats of the Cold War and in countering emerging threats to the security of the United States," cited in *The Washington Quarterly*, vol. 20, no. 3, Summer 1997.

[19] Prime Minister Manmohan Singh's statement in the *Lok Sabha*, (Lower House of the Indian Parliament) on Civil Nuclear Energy Cooperation with the United States, August 13, 2007 , http://pmindia.nic.in/lspeech.asp?id=569

[20] Nitin Pai and Aruna Urs, "Interview: The New Currency of Power – A Discussion on Strategic Affairs with K Subrahmanyam," *Pragati–The Indian National Interest Review*, May 2008.

in vigorously supporting total nuclear disarmament even as it is gradually putting in place an effective deterrent for reasons of national security. Its adherence to the spirit of the NPT and the CTBT has been exemplary, even though it chooses not to sign these unequal treaties.

Pakistan

Pakistan considers nuclear weapons as its most prized strategic asset and along with the Pakistan army, as the ultimate guarantor of its integrity as a nation-state. Pakistan's policies stem from its anti-India fixation and its apprehension that India is somehow working towards its dismemberment. Pakistan's General Mirza Aslam Beg had stated when he was the COAS: "Oxygen is basic to life, and one does not debate its desirability; 'nuclear deterrence' has assumed that life-saving property for Pakistan."[21] Pakistan's nuclear weapons are wholly and solely India-centric—a fact underlined by the statement of former Pakistani Foreign Minister, Abdul Sattar, when he asserted:[22]

> ... No issue is more vital for the security of Pakistan than what should be Pakistan's strategy in the face of India's declaration of intent to build a massive arsenal of nuclear weapons and delivery systems... In the absence of alternatives, acquisition of the nuclear option was conceived as a means of deterrence... Minimum nuclear deterrence will remain the guiding principle of our nuclear strategy.

---

[21] General Mirza Aslam Beg, "Pakistan's Nuclear Imperatives," *Development and Security Thoughts and R eflections,* National Dev elopment and S ecurity, v ol. 3, no. 2, November 1994.

[22] Statement on "Pakistan 's Response to the Indian Nuclear Doctrine," by Pakistan 's Foreign Minister, Abdul Sat tar, cited in *Disarmament Diplomacy,* no. 41, November 1999.

Pakistan's nuclear weapons are seen as a means to counter India's conventional superiority. Thus, deterrence has been used by Pakistan to neutralise the possibility of an Indian conventional attack even while pursuing revisionist policies itself.[23]

The better part of the UN disarmament conference in 2009 was stuck in procedural wrangles raised by Pakistan, suggesting that 2010 also marked another year of halting progress. Though Pakistan, a non-signatory to the NPT, has agreed to participate in negotiations on the FMCT, it opposes the FMCT on the grounds that it must cover reduction of existing stocks of fissile materials to be truly effective. This is obviously to prevent a permanent armament gap vis-à-vis India. According to Pakistan's former Foreign Secretary, Shamshad Ahmad, attempts to set aside the principle of verification to cater to some specific interests were being made vis-à-vis a verifiable FMCT. For Pakistan, incorporation of international and effective verification into an FMCT mandate is of critical importance. Ahmad further accused India of having "linked its concurrence on joining the negotiations on FMCT to its perspective that the scope of the treaty would be limited to the 'cut-off' of future production of fissile material only."[24] Apparently this is a key issue on which India finds itself in complete agreement with other major NWS.

---

[23] Views expressed by PR Chari and Manpreet Sethi during a Workshop on Nuclear Disarmament and R egional Securit y, or ganised by the Institute f or Peace and Conflict Studies, August 2008; for more on this subject also see, Peter Lav oy, "Pakistan's Nuclear P osture: Security and Surviv ability," R eport by the Nonpr oliferation Policy Education Center, January 2007 , pp. 4-5.

[24] Shamshad Ahmad, "Disarmament Concerns and P akistan," *The Dawn*, September 5, 2009.

Islamabad appears wary of the proposed focus in the programme on limiting the production of fissile material, which would put it at a disadvantage against longer-standing nuclear powers, most significantly India. It, therefore, has an interest in delaying the start of substantive talks. The Pakistani Ambassador at the conference, Zamir Akram, had stated that Islamabad did not want to work with a programme that was 'frozen in time' and took the floor to call for the agenda to be broadened to cover two additional issues: conventional arms control at the regional and sub-regional level; and a global regime on all aspects of missiles.[25] Reaching a consensus on these issues is likely to be complicated, since India has rejected a discussion of regional conventional arms control arguing that the conference should focus on global issues instead. This is yet another concerted effort by Pakistan to include regional arms control directed against its conventionally superior adversary.

Pakistan is willing to give up its nuclear weapons provided India does the same; it has linked negotiations on the FMCT to a reduction in the existing stocks of fissile material and has yet to demonstrate credible curbs on the non-proliferation activities of the state as well as rogue members of its nuclear establishment like Dr. A Q Khan. Hence, Pakistan's disarmament and non-proliferation track record continues to provide cause for concern.

Israel

The international community had reluctantly accepted Israel's status as a state with nuclear weapons (SNW) when the US

---

[25] For more details see statement by Ambassador Zamir Akram at the Plenary Meeting, United Nations Office at Geneva, January 2010.

intelligence community hinted at the same in July 1970.[26] With no known nuclear doctrine and choosing to remain outside the NPT fold, Israel refuses to confirm or deny its nuclear status. Although Israel voted in favour of UN General Assembly Resolution 2373 of 1968 adopting the NPT, Jerusalem does not find in the NPT adequate protection for own security tribulations and regional concerns.

Ever since former Israeli Prime Minister, Levi Eshkol pledged in the mid-1960s that Israel would not be the first nation to introduce nuclear weapons to the West Asia, Israel's subsequent leaders have also adhered to this opaque declaratory policy. Notwithstanding this facet, a marked lacuna exists in its policy on arms control and disarmament are concerned, much in contrast to the availability of extensive literature focusing on its policy of nuclear opacity. In the decades since the 1970s, this visible opacity has given Israel credible nuclear deterrence at negligible political cost. In July 2007, the Israeli Atomic Energy Commission provided limited and non-specific details regarding the Israeli civilian nuclear programme. Although Israel does support a non-discriminatory and verifiable FMCT, it maintains that the treaty should not cover existing stockpiles. Further, Israel continues to assert its vehement opposition to issues pertaining to disarmament until after a 'comprehensive West Asia peace agreement' has been arrived at. While visiting Israel in mid-2007, International Atomic Energy Agency (IAEA) Director-General, Mohamed ElBaradei, expressed concern over Israel's refusal to sign the NPT given that

---

[26] Hedrick Smith, "US Assumes the Israelis Have A-Bomb or its Parts," *The New York Times*, July 18, 1970.

it would undermine the treaty's legitimacy, particularly in the Arab public opinion.[27]

Israel was accepted as a full member of the CD in June 1996 and subsequently joined the founding signatory states of the convention that forbids the development, production, stockpiling and use of chemical weapons and mandates their complete destruction (CWC).[28] While expressing concern over the Iranian nuclear pursuit, Israel's Ambassador, Eytan Bentsur stated in the CD that Tehran is currently engaged in acquiring non-conventional capabilities, in a manner which is not consistent with its international obligations. He urged the international community to prevent such dangerous developments; which are likely to further de-stabilise the West Asia. Further, Israel has also laid stress on maintaining a balance between verification regimes and their steadfast compliance.[29] On the other hand, Ali Larijani, speaker of the Iranian Parliament- *Majlis*, censured Israeli possession of hundreds of nuclear warheads and urged countries across the globe to work collectively to rid the world of nuclear weapons.[30] This rhetoric evidently leads to the conclusion that the possibility of a nuclear freeze in politically volatile West Asia does not seem likely in the near future and that any tangible

---

[27] Mohamed ElBaradei, "Israel Impedes Nuclear Disarmament," *International Herald Tribune*, February 2009.

[28] "Israel Joins UN Disarmament Committee," Release by the Israel Ministry of Foreign Affairs, Jerusalem, June 19, 1996.

[29] "Israel's Approach to Regional Security, Arms Control and Disarmament, " Statement by Director General of Israel's Ministry of Foreign Affairs, Ambassador Eytan Bentsur, Before the Conference on Disarmament, Geneva, September 4, 1997.

[30] "Iran slams Israel's Atomic Warheads, Vows Disarmament," *Iranian Press TV* report, February 27, 2010.

breakthrough in the CD appears highly improbable. Alireza Moaiyeri, Iranian ambassador to the UN, addressed the CD and enunciated the primary goal of the CD to , "... remove insecurity and to establish a world free of nuclear weapons." Moaiyeri affirmed that Tehran supported the start of talks on a FMCT, though the pact should cover existing stocks of fissile material as well as their future production. Tehran also supports negotiations on preventing an arms race in outer space and on a legally binding instrument to provide security assurances to all NNWS.[31]

Significantly, a mere 72 hours prior to completing its two-year term in the UN Security Council, Syria (an NPT signatory state since 1969) formally introduced a resolution in December 2003 calling for a Nuclear-Weapon-Free Zone (NWFZ) in West Asia despite of the fact that Syria is suspected of harbouring nuclear weapons ambitions itself. It was widely speculated that the 2003 resolution was prompted by Libya's decision when it decided to come clean on its WMD programme.[32] Libya divested itself of its nuclear weapons programme in December 2003 when it agreed to eliminate all materials, equipment and programmes resulting in the production of nuclear or other internationally proscribed weapons. While violating obligations of the NPT by virtue of being a signatory, Libya, under the leadership of Mu'ammar al-Gaddafi admitted that it had pursued a nuclear weapons programme, purportedly to counter the covert Israeli nuclear arsenal.

---

[31] "Iran envoy calls for global nuclear disarmament," *Reuters News*, February 19, 2009.

[32] "Disarmament: Syria Asks Nuclear-free West Asia (Israel, That Is)" *Thalif Deen*, (Inter Press Service English News Wire), December 12, 2003.

Clearly, Israel's ambiguity on the possession of nuclear weapons and its proclaimed doctrine that it will not be the first to use nuclear weapons and nor will be the last, have undermined strategic stability in West Asia as well as the non-proliferation regime. In the near future, Israel is unlikely to change its stance and, therefore, continuing volatility may be expected in West Asia. Nations in Israel's neighbourhood like Iraq in the past and Iran and Syria today, and perhaps others in future, may be expected to continue to harbour nuclear ambitions as they find Israel's possession of nuclear weapons and its belligerence to be threatening.

North Korea

At the turn of the millennium, the Democratic People's Republic of Korea (DPRK) set off a crisis with its admission of an active nuclear weapons programme in October 2002, in violation of the 1994 Agreed Framework with the US. Though North Korea's nuclear programme started well before 1985, it was only after it joined the NPT in the same year that global attention was focused on its nuclear activities. Subsequently, as the IAEA demanded by means of its resolutions that North Korea return to compliance, Pyongyang announced its withdrawal from the NPT on January 10, 2003.[33] The crisis over North Korea's nuclear programme made it evident that the global non-proliferation regime, long symbolised by the NPT was inescapably breaking down. On the contrary, the 2006 International Weapons of Mass Destruction Commission report titled, 'Weapons of Terror,' suggested that contrary to what was often being attributed to the NPT regime

---

[33] Victor Cha, "Mr Koizumi goes to Pyongyang,"*Comparative Connections,* October 2002, available at http://www.csis.org/pacfor/cc/0203Qjapan_skorea.htm

regarding the possibility wherein it risks collapse, both Libya and Iraq that were found to be in violation of the treaty were subsequently brought back into observance.[34]

It had become increasingly clear that North Korea's revived nuclear programme was consistent with its attempts to acquire a bargaining plank with the US as well as with other key adversaries in East Asia. As North Korea declared itself a nuclear weapons power in October 2006, the orientation of the existing strategic equation in Northeast Asia changed drastically. There were strong arguments that proliferation cases were likely to get only tougher, with Iran taking its cues from the North Korea case study. All this while, Iran's nuclear quagmire continued unabated and IAEA Director-General, Mohamed ElBaradei stating that Iran was not cooperating with UN inspectors. Significantly, failure in case of resolving the Iranian nuclear quagmire could well create serious risks of escalation coupled with long-term domino effects.

Nevertheless, on the face of it, North Korean leader Kim Jong II in a meeting with Chinese Communist Party official at that point of time, Wang Jiarui, reiterated his country's 'persistent stance to realise the de-nuclearisation' of the Korean peninsula.[35] It should be noted that North Korea insists that sanctions be lifted before it returns to disarmament talks. On the other hand, Washington continues to maintain that Pyongyang must return to the negotiating table before any talk on political and economic concessions. It is implausible that Pyongyang shall surrender its

---

[34] For more details on this report see, Hans Blix, "Nuclear Freeze: The West Asia and Global Arms Contr ol," *Boston Review*, May/June 2007.

[35] "North Korea's Kim said to Pledge Nuclear Disarmament", *The Associated Press*, February 8, 2010.

nuclear card so easily. The North Korean leadership is unlikely to take the road to complete disarmament and relinquish its nuclear capabilities in totality unless it secures massive economic bargains as well as security guarantees for itself.

Conclusion

Given its outstanding non-proliferation track record, India has been accepted as a de facto SNW outside the NPT by the international community, including the Nuclear Suppliers Group (NSG). It has also signed a safeguards agreement with the IAEA and is now on its way to entering into contracts for the supply of reactor technology and nuclear fuel for civilian nuclear energy use. However, given its dismal proliferation record and the heightened risk of its nuclear weapons falling into *Jihadi* hands, Pakistan poses the greatest near-term challenge to the non-proliferation regime – with the sole exception of North Korea, whose deviant behavior is perplexing as well as distressing. Iran's continuing intransigence has ushered in a fresh round of UN sanctions which will hurt its economy in the long run. Its stubborn resistance to IAEA inspections – even while it denies any nuclear weapons ambitions – may also lead eventually to US-Israel military strikes against its nuclear facilities. Israel's possession of nuclear weapons will continue to undermine confidence in the non-proliferation regime in West Asia.

As the world ponders over the issue of the slow pace of nuclear disarmament, the continuing activities of most of the SNW outside the NPT fold paint a dismal picture. For these nations, their limited nuclear arsenal serves as a very crucial political tool and bargaining chip owing to the fluid regional security situation. The noted scholar George Perkovich has argued that nuclear disarmament and resolution of political–security conflicts would have to proceed together in a reciprocating, co-evolutionary process. A gradual reduction in the nuclear arsenals of the NWS can potentially facilitate other states to support a strengthened non-proliferation regime, but it would have to occur in a non-discriminatory fashion.

If the vision of a nuclear weapons free world has to be brought to fruition, the onus certainly lies on the major nuclear powers. The United States must take the lead in the move towards complete nuclear disarmament. Only then will the idea of a world free of the scourge of nuclear weapons take root. President Barack Obama had electrified the aspirations of the world's youth to move towards nuclear disarmament with his speech at Prague in 2009. It is to be hoped that he will be able to give substance to his lofty ideals during his remaining term in office and not get bogged down in day-to-day domestic issues like the oil spill in the Gulf of Mexico. Countries like India must remain firm in their support for the elimination of nuclear weapons.

US - RUSSIA NUCLEAR ARSENAL REDUCTION : A EUROPEAN PERSPECTIVE

Lukasz Kulesa

European countries were assumed to be the natural allies of the United States in the promotion and implementation of the agenda of global nuclear disarmament, which was set out by President Barack Obama in April 2009 in Prague. The aim of abolishing nuclear weapons has been advocated by many Europeans even at the high point of the Cold War, although these weapons were at the same time contributing significantly to the "cold peace" between NATO and the Warsaw Pact, and relative stability of the situation in Europe between 1945 and 1989. Later on, after the breakup of the Soviet Union, the prevailing view in Europe was that nuclear weapons have no positive impact on security, and the European comity of states can function in the XXI century without nuclear deterrence. The resistance in a number of major European countries to the assertive security policy of George W. Bush (including the development of the new types of nuclear weapons and the Missile Defence project), seemed to signal that Europe prefers a world in which the brute force, including the nuclear weapons, would have no place in international relations.

These factors, taken together with the popularity of the recently elected US President Barack Obama in Europe, should have made the European countries strong and clear-voiced supporters of the new disarmament policy. Yet, in a paper summing up the implementation of the Obama agenda one year after the Prague speech, George Perkovich lists among the "difficult issues" the position of a European country - France, which, according to him, expresses 'doubts about the desirability and feasibility of raising expectations regarding nuclear disarmament'.[1] He also mentions the Eastern European NATO members' anxiety over the value of US extended nuclear deterrence as a factor impeding the progress on the US initiative. It seems that instead of wholehearted support from Europe, the United States is facing resistance from within the ranks of its closest allies.

The explanation to this apparent paradox lies in the examination of Europe's views on the nuclear arsenals of the United States and Russia, and its significance for the security of the continent. Whereas there is a universal agreement in Europe that the reductions of the both countries' arsenals and the operational readiness of their forces would be a positive factor for the global as well as European security, disagreements emerge about the specific points on the global zero agenda. Some question the feasibility or wisdom of the nuclear disarmament as such, others point out that moving towards this goal could expose Europe to new vulnerabilities, while offering little in return. An important question for Europe is also how to support the

---

[1] George Perkovich, *The Obama Nuclear Agenda One Year after Prague,* Carnegie Endowment for International Peace, Policy Outlook, March 31, 2010.

reductions in nuclear weapons, without jeopardizing its security interests or assuming the role of a junior follower of the US and Russia.

For India, which has emerged early on as a supporter of universal nuclear disarmament, the understanding of the forces shaping the European position on this subject might be helpful in shaping its own policy. The European Union is often perceived as an actor which pursues an idealistic agenda in international relations, including a wholehearted support for the nuclear disarmament. In fact, within Europe this idealistic approach frequently clashes with a more realistic reading of international relations, one in which nuclear weapons continue to play a role in assuring the security of the continent against external challenges. In this context, parallels can probably be drawn between the position of Europe and the Indian debate on the relationship between the support for disarmament, and the requirements for maintaining minimum credible deterrence posture.

Nuclear Weapons - the (un)importance of Europe

Historically, Europe has not been a player, but rather a battleground for the US – Soviet nuclear confrontation. During the Cold War, both NATO and the Soviet-dominated Warsaw Pact prepared for a war in Europe, which (according to the military planners of both sides) would have a nuclear dimension. In addition to the strategic forces, tactical (sub-strategic) nuclear weapons were deployed in Europe and were supposed to be used from the beginning of such a conflict. At the highest point during the Cold War, NATO had at its disposal approximately 7000 tactical nuclear warheads with prepared delivery systems, while the Warsaw Pact had about 10000 warheads. Fully aware of the fact that in the event of war, the European territory would suffer unimaginable levels of destruction, the European populations and their leadership developed a somehow ambivalent attitude towards the nuclear weapons. On the one hand, strong anti-nuclear NGOs and social movements demanded nuclear abolition, and European leaders frequently expressed their support for the goal of a nuclear-free Europe. On the other hand, many tacitly recognized that the nuclear deterrence, backed by the large nuclear arsenals and the deployment of nuclear forces in Europe, provided a shield against the start of hostilities between the two camps. In this sense, the European post-Second World War recovery and economic development was made possible by the stability brought by the nuclear weapons of the United States and the Soviet Union.

After the end of the Cold War, the easing of tensions and significant nuclear forces reductions agreed by the United States and Russia were met with enthusiasm in Europe. The Europeans welcomed specifically the withdrawal of the majority of tactical nuclear weapons from the continent to Russia and the United States. The nuclear weapons of the United Kingdom and France were also scaled down significantly. At the same time, it should be noted that Europe quickly focused on other priorities (in the security domain, primarily on managing the consequences of the breakup of Yugoslavia and NATO enlargement), while the issues of nuclear weapons, arms reductions and disarmament received little attention. Specifically, virtually no pressure was applied on Great Britain or France to relinquish their arsenals.

The renewal of interest in nuclear disarmament came after the 2007 initiative of Henry Kissinger, Sam Nunn, William Perry and George Schultz.[2] Former senior decision-makers and politicians from the United Kingdom, Germany, Italy, Poland, France, the Netherland and Belgium responded to this call by declaring their support for the vision of the world without nuclear weapons.[3] They also called for their own countries and other European partners to support this goal and to actively work towards its fulfillment. It should be noted that the Europeans underlined the principal responsibility of the United States and Russia for the progress on nuclear disarmament, but stressed that Europe should assume part of the responsibility.

The majority of the European governments backed the goal of the world without nuclear weapons, as it became a part of the agenda of the new US Presidential administration of Barack Obama. The European countries rightly assessed that this issue will be vigorously pursued by the US president, and in official

[2] Henry Kissinger, Sam Nunn, William P erry, George Schultz, 'A World Free of Nuclear Weapons', *Wall Street Journal,* 4 January 2007.

[3] Douglas Hurd, Malcolm Rifkind, David Owen and George Robertson, 'Start worrying and learn to ditch the bomb' , *The Times,* 30 June 2008; Massimo D'Alema, Gianfranco Fini, Giorgio La Malfa, Arturo Parisi, Francesco Calogero, 'Per un mondo senza armi nucleari' , *Corriere della Sera,* 24 July 2008; Egon Bahr, Hans-Dietrich Genscher, Helmut Schmidt, Richard von Weizsäcker, 'Toward a nuclear-free world: a German view', *International Herald Tribune,* 9 January 2009; Aleksander K waœniewski, Tadeusz Maz owiecki, Lech W a³êsa, 'Œwiat bez broni j¹drowej', *Gazeta Wyborcza,* 3 April 2009; Alain Juppé, B ernard Norlain, Alain Richard, Michel Rocard, 'Pour un désarmement nuclé aire mondial, seule réponse à la prolifération anarchique' , *le Monde,* 14 October 2009; Ruud Lubbers, Max van der Stoel, Hans van Mierlo, Frits Korthals Altes,'Op naar een k ernwapenvrije wereld' ['T oward a nuclear weapon f ree world'], *Handelsblad,* 23 November 2009; Willy Claes, Jean-Luc Dehaene, Louis Michel, Guy V erhofstadt, 'V ers un monde sans armes nucleaires', *De Standaard,* 19 February 2010.

pronouncements declared their readiness to take part in the process. Also, the disarmament rhetoric energized the European activists and organizations advocating this goal, especially in Western Europe.

At the same time, the Europeans are aware of their limited influence over the non-European nuclear weapon states. The European position can be considered of little importance when compared with the challenges of bringing down the numbers of the Russian and US nuclear weapons, de-nuclearising North Korea, containing the Chinese nuclear policy, or bringing into the disarmament process the non-NPT countries: India, Pakistan, and Israel. Still, the attitudes of the European states towards the concept of nuclear disarmament have an impact on the assessment of the feasibility of the project.

US and Russian Nuclear Weapons from a European Perspective

Europeans almost never fail to note that the nuclear arsenals of the United States and Russia represent more than 90% of the global nuclear warhead stockpile. The size and composition of the arsenals are a direct legacy of the Cold War, and from the European point of view they are unjustified by the security needs or threat level of neither US nor Russia. The importance which the two countries attach to nuclear deterrence seems for Europe, out of sync with the security challenges of the 21st century, where asymmetric threats and challenges cannot be successfully countered with the threat of nuclear retaliation. Whereas in other regions of the world, including East Asia and the Indian subcontinent, nuclear deterrence plays an important role in interstate relations, for mainstream European thinking it appears to be an outdated conceptual framework for managing relations with its neighbours, and even its potential opponents.

It should not be implied, however, that Europe underestimates the threat caused by nuclear weapons. On the contrary, the 2003 European Union Security Strategy described the proliferation of the weapons of mass destruction as 'potentially the greatest threat' to the European security.[4] The report of the implementation of the Strategy, adopted by the EU in 2008, repeats that assessment, adding that the risk of negative consequences of nuclear proliferation for the EU has increased since 2003. Still, the EU documents do not declare that the possession of the nuclear weapons or nuclear deterrence can provide a shield against the proliferators or possessors of nuclear weapons. The relationship may even be constructed as the opposite: the continued reliance on huge nuclear stockpiles by the nuclear weapons states is an obstacle in discouraging other countries from acquiring nuclear arsenals.

Whereas in the Cold War era the possibility of a NATO-Soviet nuclear confrontation in Europe was included in the security thinking of the countries in the continent, currently the Russian (or US) nuclear capabilities are not viewed in terms of a direct security threat to Europe. Instead, the primary concern of the European states has to do more with the uncertainty regarding the security and safety conditions of storing the nuclear weapons and materials on Russian territory. Especially for the sub-strategic (tactical) nuclear weapons, there is only a basic level of knowledge about their operational status, locations and modes of storage and deployment, and the security arrangements preventing accidents or theft. For example, it is unclear whether all Russian weapons are equipped with devices preventing un-authorized use.

---

[4] 'A Secure Europe in a Better World, European Security Strategy', EU Security Strategy, Brussels, 12 December 2003, p. 3.

These factors are much less worrying with regard to Russian strategic nuclear weapons, which have been the focus of substantial investments aimed at assuring their reliability and security (financed by Russia or through the US-Russian Nunn-Lugar programme).

Similar concerns, albeit on a much smaller scale, have been expressed about the US tactical nuclear weapons stored on European territory. Coming after the much-publicized incident of mishandling of nuclear-armed cruise missiles in the United States, an official US report (*Air Force Blue Ribbon Review of Nuclear Weapons Policies*) highlighted in February 2008 that security levels at bases in Europe where US nuclear weapons were stored, varied from country to country. Even though the report did not reveal any serious flaws, it drove attention to the fact that US weapons in Europe might also be targets for attack or theft. In 2003, a terrorist plot was discovered to attack the Belgian base at Kleine Brogel, and in 2010 a group of peace activists penetrated the perimeter of the same base (even though NATO and Belgian authorities insisted that they did not manage to breach the security in the area of the base where nuclear weapons are reportedly stored).[5]

The concerns over safety and security of the Russian and US weapons seem to be much more vivid than any anxieties about the threat which these weapons may directly cause for Europe. Taken the close transatlantic relations and the partnership in NATO, any form of hostility between Europe and the US can be dismissed out of hand. The Europeans worry more about the

---

[5] 'Peace Activists Trespass at Belgian Base Housing U.S. Nukes', Global Security Newswire, February 17, 2010.

possible consequences of the US's willingness to use nuclear weapons in the vicinity of the continent. Especially during the presidency of George W. Bush, when various ideas were floated for a new generation of low-yield weapons, which could be used to strike deep-buried targets and WMD storage sites (e.g. the Robust Nuclear Earth Penetrator), the reaction from Europe was overly negative. It was argued that the United States is not only harming its non-proliferation goals by appearing to lower the threshold for the use of nuclear weapons, but also endangering its allies, who may bear the consequences of transforming a conventional conflict into a nuclear one by the use of the new weapons.

With regard to Russia as a nuclear threat, the opinions in Europe vary. While recognizing that the Russian potential to deliver devastating blows to European territory and populations, the Europeans tend to agree that Russia would be extremely hesitant to use nuclear weapons as an instrument of blackmail or coercion in any political confrontation. Despite the occasional crises in the relations with Russia, the mutual interdependence seems to be too high to make the resort to the nuclear argument attractive to Russia. In fact, the only time in recent years when a reference was made to the nuclear weapons as an instrument of coercion came in the context of the debate over the deployments of the elements of the US Missile Defence system in Poland and the Czech Republic. The head of the Russian nuclear strategic forces warned in 2007 that if the deployments proceeded as planned, Russia could include these installations in the list of targets for its nuclear forces.[6] However, instead of forcing the countries concerned to reconsider their policies, such a statement only increased their determination to move forward with the deployment. Throughout Europe, Russia's threats were considered a propaganda stunt, unhelpful in resolving the crisis over Missile Defence deployment in Central Europe.

Still, the fact that Russia historically treated Central and Eastern European countries – now members of NATO and the European Union – as its own sphere of influence, combined with the recent assertiveness of Moscow in the conduct of the foreign policy (as evidenced e.g. by the Georgian-Russian war of 2008), provides the background for the continued support of a number of European countries for maintaining the nuclear dimension of NATO and specifically, for the provision of nuclear extended deterrence by the United States. As put in the 1999 Strategic Concept of the Alliance, "Nuclear weapons make a unique contribution in rendering the risks of aggression against the Alliance incalculable and unacceptable".[7] The same document also sanctions the stationing of the US nuclear forces in Europe, stipulating that "Nuclear forces based in Europe and committed to NATO provide an essential political and military link between the European and the North American members of the Alliance". Even though no European country would openly argue for the need to keep the US nuclear forces in Europe as a potential deterrent against Russia, such opinions are sometimes expressed privately. According to the May 2009 report of the Congressional Commission on the Strategic Posture of the United States (the

---

[6] 'US missi le shield' "could be tar get", *Al Jazeera,* February 20, 2007, ht tp://
english.aljazeera.net/news/europe/2007/02/2008525123124554344.html.

[7] 'Str ategic Concept', Appr oved b y the Heads of State and Go vernment
participating in the meeting of the North Atlantic Council in Washington D.C.
on 23rd and 24th April 1999.

so-called Perry-Schlesinger Commission), "some allies located near Russia believe that U.S. non-strategic forces in Europe are essential to prevent nuclear coercion by Moscow, and indeed that modernized U.S./NATO forces are essential for restoring a sense of balance in the face of Russia's nuclear renewal".[8] Consequently, the possible reductions of the US nuclear arsenal which would involve the sub-strategic weapons meets with resistance from some of the European countries.

As evidenced already, the existence of the nuclear arsenals of the United States and Russia is not universally condemned by the Europeans. The stability and security brought by nuclear weapons is highlighted by some members of the strategic community and linked with the observation that they make major wars between the great powers "highly unlikely".[9] Such a situation, it can be implied, suits Europe, which otherwise might be forced to increase its military expenditure and possibly become involved in the power struggle between Russia and the United States. From that point of view, it is in the vital interest of Europe to support the maintenance of strategic balance between the two superpowers. Additionally, when US and Russia cooperate on the reductions of their nuclear arsenals, it creates positive momentum for US – Russian relations, which in turn has a "spillover effect" on Europe -Russia relations. If, on the other hand, the elements of rivalry dominate the bilateral US-Russian nuclear agenda, Europe can easily become a victim of such

---

[8] 'America's Strategic Posture', the Final Report of the Congressional Commission on the Strategic Posture of the Untied States, US Institute for Peace, Washington D.C. 2009, p.20.

[9] B. Tertrais, "The Illogic of Zero", *The Washington Quarterly*, April 2010, p. 127.

competition, with the most recent example being the controversy over US plans to develop Missile Defence in Europe.

The final point on the utility of US and Russian nuclear weapons concerns the two European nuclear weapon states. These two countries' arsenals vastly exceed the nuclear holdings of France and the United Kingdom, the former have at their disposal a strong argument for resisting further cuts and calls for unilateral disarmament. In that sense, the vast numbers of the nuclear weapons possessed by the two nuclear superpowers shield the European nuclear weapon states from criticism. As long as they do not reach low numbers of warheads and delivery systems, the UK and France can point to them as a reason for holding on to their own nuclear arsenals.

How can the European Union contribute to further reductions in US and Russian Nuclear arsenals?

The strong moral and political support expressed by the European leaders and experts for the new START treaty, signed by the presidents of Russia and the United States in Prague in April 2010, reflected genuine appreciation of the success reached by both parties.[10] Still, while it is universally recognized that the US and Russia would remain engaged in bilateral negotiations over the next round of cuts in their arsenals, it is also pointed out that the European Union may to some extent contribute to the process of further reductions.

Europe can certainly facilitate further cuts by contributing to the strengthening of the nuclear non-proliferation regime and to the easing of the international non-proliferation crises. In the

---

[10] See e.g. J.P. Zanders, 'A Good START', ISS EU Analysis, April 2010.

discussions over the feasibility of moving towards the world free of nuclear weapons, one re-occurring theme is the need to secure a strong system of monitoring compliance and dealing with the proliferation challenges. It is argued that unless the nuclear weapon countries have a high degree of confidence that other states would not be able to clandestinely produce nuclear weapons, they would not decide on deeper reductions of their own arsenals. The potential of the EU to act towards re-assuring the nuclear weapon states, first of all the United States and Russia, that their security would not be diminished in the process of disarmament, is significant.

The European Union attempts to establish itself as an intermediary, a bridge between the nuclear weapon states and the countries and groups interested in more significant progress towards nuclear disarmament. As an organization which groups together two nuclear weapon states (UK and France), a number of countries which are members of NATO and take part in the nuclear planning of the Alliance, and also non-NATO countries with a strong pro-disarmament position (Sweden, Austria, Ireland), the European Union is a body which formulates its policy on a basis of a compromise between the nuclear weapons possessors and opponents. As such, the presence of the UK and France at the table during the EU's decision making process can serve as a guarantee for other nuclear weapon states that its position takes their interests into account. Also, the EU, with its 27 member states and considerable demographic, political and economic power, is regarded as an important actor by other members of the non-proliferation regimes. Helpful in establishing the EU's reputation have been measures such as disseminating common positions for the international conferences (including the NPT Review Conferences), financing cooperative programs to eliminate dangerous materials and weapon components, or strengthening institutional and physical capacity of partners to deal with proliferation challenges.

The countries of the European Union attempt to be active in resolving the proliferation crises which has an impact on the attitude of the nuclear weapon states towards the disarmament. The Iranian nuclear crisis is considered here by the Europeans as a crucial factor in determining the future of 'global zero'. If Iran decides to cross the nuclear threshold, it will create incentives for other countries in the region to move along a similar path, and reinforce the argument that only nuclear deterrence can provide defence against such a threat.

This factor adds additional urgency to the European diplomatic efforts aimed at defusing the crisis. After the exposure of the scope of the Iranian programme in 2002, the three European countries (France, Germany and the UK) attempted direct negotiations with Teheran. Later, they joined other members of the Security Council in the P5+1 group, which made several attempts to bring a negotiated solution to the confrontation. According to the last such proposal, formulated in 2009 and rejected by Teheran, Iran was to swap its low-enriched uranium for the fuel for its research nuclear reactor in Teheran. France was supposed to be one of the countries offering to manufacture the fuel rods for this purpose. The actions of the EU-3 group has been supported by the European Union as a whole, which imposed several rounds of sanctions on Iran, including the ones going beyond the provisions of the relevant Security Council resolutions.

The last option for the European Union to impact the policies of the US and Russia consists of applying direct diplomatic pressure. In its Common Position for the 2010 NPT Review Conference, the EU members noted the "special responsibility" of the states with the largest arsenals of nuclear weapons in the fulfillment of the obligations of Article VI of the NPT.[11] Also, while welcoming the new START agreement between the United States and the Russian Federation, they stressed "the need for more progress in decreasing their arsenals and in reducing the operational readiness of their nuclear weapon systems to the minimum level necessary". Still, it needs to be noted that the weight of such statements is quite weak. The European states refrain from criticizing in a more direct way on the slow process of nuclear reductions of US and Russia. In fact, the EU documents avoid referring directly to the global zero agenda, speaking instead about working towards creating "the conditions for a world without nuclear weapons".[12] Such an approach is directly connected with a resistance inside the EU, most notably from France, to align the organization with the radical agenda of nuclear disarmament. Instead of that, the EU opts for a more incremental approach, in which nuclear disarmament is reached not through applying pressure on the nuclear weapon states, but rather through cooperating with them to remove some of the obstacles preventing them for changing their nuclear policy.

---

[11] Council Decision 2010/212/CFSP of 29 March 2010, relating to the position of the European Union for the 2010 Review Conference of the Parties to the NPT, published 10 April 2010.

[12] 'Statement on behalf of the European Union by H.E. Catherine Ashton, High Representative of the European Union', at the General Debate of the Review Conference of the NPT, 3 May 2010.

The Role for NATO: Phasing out Nuclear Extended Deterrence?

Whereas the European Union can directly do little to influence the nuclear policies of the US and Russia, the European states which are members of NATO are faced with a dilemma which is closely related to the future of the nuclear arsenals of the two superpowers. As mentioned above, the North Atlantic Alliance has at its disposal between 150 and 240 US tactical nuclear weapons (B-61 gravity bombs), stationed in six bases in Belgium, the Netherlands, Germany, Italy and Turkey.[13] NATO members, Belgium, the Netherlands, Germany and Italy participate in the nuclear-sharing arrangements with the US, which involves the deployment of the dual-capable aircraft (F-16 and Tornado), modified and certified to deliver US nuclear gravity bombs. The weapons assigned to NATO missions can also be in some cases delivered by US aircraft. The status of Greece and Turkey, as regard the nuclear missions for their air forces, remains unclear.[14] As for the other NATO members (except for France), they take part in the Nuclear Planning Group, which supervises this aspect of NATO policy. Russia, for its part, reveals little information about its arsenal of the sub-strategic weapons and their storage sites. It is estimated, however, that Moscow may have as much as 5,390 sub-strategic warheads, with approximately one third of

---

[13] Hans Kristensen, 'Status of U .S. Nuclear W eapons in Eur ope', Federation of Atomic Scientists, 26 June, 2008. See: http://www.fas.org/programs/ssp/nukes/_images/EuroNukes.pdf.

[14] For a detailed description of the state of knowledge about the deployment and DCA capabilities, see: Ian Anthony, *The Future of Nuclear Weapons in NATO*, Friedrich Ebert Stiftung, 2008, pp. 26-32; and Hans Kristensen's blog entries at http://www.fas.org/blog/ssp/category/hans_kristensen.

them operational and the rest inactive or held in reserve[15].

A number of European countries have recently called for a change in NATO policy. It is argued that by sending a strong signal to the United States about the readiness of its European partners to stop relying on the nuclear extended deterrence based on the sub-strategic systems, they can bring about a change in the US nuclear posture, and possibly also in the Russian one. If the presence of the sub-strategic nuclear weapons in Europe is no longer needed, the argument goes, Washington could withdraw them from the European territory. This, in turn, would open the way for the inclusion of this category of weaponry in the next round of the bilateral US-Russian arms control talks, with their elimination as the final goal. According to the supporters of this plan, Europe can thus signal a changed attitude towards the utility of nuclear weapons for NATO in the XXI century, which should be received well by other members of the international community.

The initiative of the new German government of FDP and CDU/CSU, which requested consultations in NATO and with the US on the removal of nuclear weapons from its territory, initiated the debate within NATO on this topic.[16] It put the issue of the withdrawal of nuclear weapons from Europe, discussed so far mainly among experts, government and NATO

---

[15] Robert S. Norris & Hans M. Kristensen, "Nuclear Notebook: Russian nuclear forces, 2009,"*Bulletin of the Atomic Scientist*, May/June 2009, vol. 65, no. 3, pp. 55–64.

[16] The pledge to pursue the withdrawal of the remaining nuclear weapons from Germany in contacts within NATO and with the US was included in the coalition agreement between the FDP and CDU/CDU from 24 October 2009. See: http://www.cdu.de/doc/pdfc/091026-koalitionsvertrag-cducsu-fdp.pdf.

officials, into the public spotlight. In February 2010, the ministers of foreign affairs of five NATO countries (Germany, Norway, Belgium, the Netherlands, Luxemburg) wrote a letter to the NATO Secretary General, Anders Fogh Rasmussen, urging him to put the issue of the change of NATO's nuclear policy on the agenda of the Alliance. They referred directly to President's Obama agenda, stressing that NATO should discuss the ways to "move closer" to the realization of the political objective of a world without nuclear weapons.

As of now, no European member of NATO has come openly in support of maintaining the US nuclear weapons on the continent. Out of record, some of the Allies in Central and Eastern Europe, as well as Turkey, expressed anxiety over the effects of a unilateral NATO move, on the grounds that it would weaken the value of US extended deterrence and the cohesion of the Alliance as a security provider.[17] A compromise solution was put forward i.a. by Poland, which together with Norway proposed addressing the issue of the sub-strategic nuclear weapons in a larger framework of European arms control. This would mean linking NATO's actions with the progress in the relations with Russia. The joint communiqué from the April 2010 meeting of the Polish and Norwegian foreign ministers suggested taking a "step-by-step approach, including transparency and confidence-building measures as well as balanced and mutual arms reductions".[18]

---

[17] Miles A. Pomper, William Potter, Nikolai Sokov, 'Reducing and Regulating Tactical (Nonstrategic) Nuclear W eapons in Eur ope', James Martin Center f or Nonproliferation Studies, Monterey Institute, Prepared for Unit for Policy Planning and Research Finnish Ministry for Foreign Affairs, December 2009,pp. 27-31.

[18] ht tp://www.psi.msz.gov.pl/files/docs/komunikaty/JOINT-STATEMENT.pdf.

The ambitious attempt of a number of European countries, strongly backed by the NGO community, to bring about a fundamental change in the Alliance's nuclear strategy and withdraw US nuclear weapons from Europe seems to have failed. The United States have accepted a more cautious approach as proposed by some of the Allies. The 2010 Nuclear Posture Review, unveiled in April 2010, highlights the political value of the weapons deployed in Europe, which "contribute to Alliance cohesion" and "provide reassurance" to some allies. It also mentions the "unique" NATO nuclear sharing arrangements. A similar position has been presented by the US representatives at the NATO meetings. Consequently, the United States have rejected calls for early unilateral withdrawal, choosing instead the track of preparing for the engagement with Russia.

Conclusion

Europe is far from united when it comes to the issue of the US and Russian nuclear weapons and their reductions. The majority of the population, and a highly motivated group of experts and politicians, believe that it is the duty of Europe to support President Obama's call for a world free of nuclear weapons. Europe should facilitate the process of the reductions of the US and Russian arsenals, as it brings closer the final steps in the process of global disarmament. Some argue that the European countries should even be prepared to move as a vanguard of the process, either through unilateral elimination of the national arsenals of France and the UK, or through changing NATO policy on the deployment of the sub-strategic weapons in Europe.

Other Europeans take a more nuanced approach. The nuclear weapons may still be perceived as a guarantee of security and stability, especially by those who value the US security umbrella over the continent. For them, any reductions in the nuclear arsenals of the two superpowers should be done in parallel and take into account the dangers caused by proliferation crises. They do not believe that unilateral gestures could change the rationale of the power politics in Europe and globally. Granted, some countries may have more parochial interests here, for example connected with the preservation of their own nuclear capabilities. Still, the arguments of the "realists", who are not moved by Obama's vision, need to be taken into account.

While approaching the new initiatives connected with Global Zero, India should take into account that even in Europe, where nuclear weapons play a marginal role in the conceptualization of its security, there have been disagreements regarding the feasibility of the project. While there is a solid agreement on the need to block further proliferation of nuclear weapons and to prevent additional countries to acquire nuclear weapons, Europe would not apply strong pressure on the countries which already have the weapons to disarm.

DETERRENCE AND DISARMAMENT

Rajesh Rajagopalan

Over the last few years, there has been a new momentum on nuclear disarmament. Though this is partly the 'Obama effect', this new interest, especially in the United States, goes back at least a decade. This is unusual because traditionally much of the demand for nuclear disarmament came from the third world or from the far left of the American political spectrum. But since the end of Cold War, nuclear disarmament has become much more of a concern among the more centrist sections of American political opinion as also among retired American military officers. This has lent certain credibility to the idea of nuclear abolition and rescued it from being a purely utopian intellectual and occasionally propagandistic exercise.

All this new enthusiasm for nuclear disarmament has not resulted in any better answers to the key problems that previous, more utopian proposals had provided. The traditional utopian answer to practical problems raised by sceptics of nuclear disarmament was a glorified appeal to the essential desirability of the end goals. Though the enthusiasm among the new converts to the religion is almost infectious and although they pay more and serious attention to some practical problems, unfortunately it is not clear that they have any better solutions. This is not to suggest that nuclear disarmament is impossible, but rather that its proponents, new and old, need to give greater credence to the international political conditions that have so far been an obstacle to nuclear disarmament.

The most critical of these obstacles is the unique capacity of nuclear weapons in deterring some kinds of threats, especially but not exclusively, the threat from other nuclear-armed powers. Nuclear deterrence is sufficiently robust that throughout the Cold War period, the US used it not just to deter direct threats against itself but extended it to deter nuclear threats against its non-nuclear allies in East Asia and Europe. Indeed, nuclear deterrence appears to work not just to deter nuclear threats, but even conventional threats because of the presumed linkage between conventional and nuclear war through the process of escalation. In other words, fear that a war that begins at the conventional level can potentially escalate to a nuclear one has prevented even conventional wars between nuclear powers. Throughout the cold war years, this fear kept the two competing great powers, the US and the Soviet Union, from controlling their behaviour strictly to prevent any possibility that their military forces might come into direct confrontation with each other. They set up elaborate rules, unique in the annals of inter-state conflict, that regulated the behaviour of their military forces to prevent any potential direct confrontation. When one side or the other inadvertently crossed these limits, both sides took swift unilateral, and sometimes cooperative action to prevent any escalation.

The new nuclear disarmament proponents accept that the challenge posed by some of the deterrence arguments need to be met. As Scott Sagan points out, the potential for nuclear breakout, the future of extended deterrence, the enforcement of disarmament, and the potential instability of small numbers, are serious issues that concern mutual nuclear disarmament: "These legitimate concerns must be addressed in a credible manner if significant progress is to be made toward the goal of a nuclear-weapons-free world."[1] In another serious effort to address the problem of nuclear disarmament, George Perkovich and James Acton begin their essay asking: "How might the security conditions which would permit nuclear weapons to be safely prohibited be created, and how might measures to implement such a prohibition be verified and enforced?"[2] Thus, for the first time, at least some proponents of nuclear disarmament are taking seriously the international political context. But though they are finally being addressed, it is argued below that proponents of nuclear disarmament have not successfully addressed these issues. International political conditions, in particular the role that nuclear deterrence plays in the maintenance of national and international security, still remains a key obstacle to progress on advancing to a true nuclear zero.

The rest of this essay is divided into three main sections. In the first section, the two main ways in which nuclear disarmament

---

[1] Scott D. Sagan, "Shared Responsibilities for Nuclear Disarmament,"in Scott D. Sagan et al, *Shared Responsibilities for Nuclear Disarmament: A Global Debate* (Cambridge, Massachusetts: American Academy of Arts and Sciences, 2010), p. 3.

[2] George Perkovich and James M. Acton (editors) *Abolishing Nuclear Weapons: A Debate* (Washington, D.C.: Carnegie Endowment for International Peace, 2009), p. 13.

advocates have addressed the issue of nuclear deterrence is examined: by either ignoring it or else by casting doubt about the benefits of nuclear deterrence. In the subsequent section, two recent proposals, one made by Scott Sagan and another by George Perkovich and James Acton is briefly addressed because these works claim to take the deterrence puzzle seriously. Finally, in the third section, some of the key international security challenges that nuclear disarmament proponents need to address are outlined, if proposals for nuclear disarmament are to be taken seriously.

Addressing the Deterrence Puzzle

Proposals for nuclear disarmament will not be credible unless they take seriously the arguments of nuclear deterrence because nuclear deterrence is the primary reason why states build and maintain nuclear weapons. While prestige may also be a motive for many states, security is the primary motive, even for states like the United Kingdom and France. Ignoring or dismissing these claims may be easy but such a dismissive attitude is likely to be reciprocated with equal disdain for nuclear disarmament proposals.

So how have nuclear disarmament proposals considered the problem of deterrence? Unfortunately, not very well. Much of the approach until now has been to either ignore the deterrence benefits of nuclear weapons completely or more often, to challenge the credibility of nuclear deterrence as strategy. Both these approaches and their flaws are illustrated below.

Ignoring Nuclear Deterrence

The strategy of ignoring the benefits of nuclear deterrence is the hallmark of the more utopian approaches to nuclear disarmament which focuses, for example, simply on future steps towards nuclear disarmament unconnected with any understanding or even acknowledgement of the political conditions that may permit or prevent progress towards nuclear disarmament. This approach has a long history, going back to the early days of the nuclear age when both the U.S. and the Soviet Union proposed steps towards total elimination and international control over nuclear weapons. Many of these proposals were deliberately designed to fail because the balance of obligations was framed in a way so as to ensure that the opposing side would reject it, making them, in essence, propaganda ploys. But many other proposals, even well-meaning ones, follow the same format by ignoring the political and security conditions necessary for progress on nuclear disarmament. The Rajiv Gandhi plan presented in June 1988 is an example if we assume that this was a well-meaning effort rather than simply a way of diverting attention from the Indian nuclear weapons programme. Asserting that "it is imperative that nuclear weapons be eliminated" the Action Plan calls for a world order based on non-violence and peaceful coexistence and "international institutions that will nurture such a world order."[3] It went on to suggest as a basis for negotiation an elaborate three stage step-by-step disarmament plan that was to be completed by 2010 whose most notable feature is its complete disconnect from any political

---

[3] "Action Plan for Ushering in a Nuclear Weapon-Free and Non-Violent World Order," Appendix 6 in Manpreet Sethi, *Nuclear Strategy: India's March Towards Credible Deterrence* (New Delhi: Centre for Air Power Studies/Knowledge World, 2009), p. 383.

or strategic context. The utopian and fantastic nature of the proposal is best illustrated in the concluding paragraph of the proposal which asserts that the "gap between the rich and poor nations will be bridged," though it does not specify if this would also be achieved by 2010.

Such proposals assume that the obvious desirability of the end-goal of nuclear disarmament is sufficient, when coupled with sincerity, to lead to nuclear disarmament. Thus, there is little consideration of why, if these were such obviously good ideas, have not so far come to pass. That these plans have not taken nuclear disarmament very far is hardly surprising, but this should also represent a warning that new proposals should be more careful in understanding rather than ignoring the political context.

Rejecting Nuclear Deterrence

An alternate approach is based on a rejection of the very idea of nuclear deterrence. This involves either or both, a rejection of the idea that nuclear deterrence has prevented war between the nuclear powers, and an assertion that even if nuclear deterrence has been successful in the case of the various Cold War confrontations, they are unlikely to be successful in the case of new nuclear powers, especially new nuclear states in the developing world.

Though these assertions usually go together, they are also sometimes made independently. For example, the so-called 'four wise men' – George P. Schultz, William J. Perry, Henry A. Kissinger and Sam Nunn – in their essay in *The Wall Street Journal* in January 2007 asserted that though nuclear weapons were "essential to maintaining international security during the cold war" dependence on nuclear weapons for the purposes of deterrence is "becoming increasingly hazardous and decreasingly effective."[4]

Most other nuclear disarmament advocates are far less kind, arguing that the logic of nuclear deterrence is itself the problem.[5] Though the latter represent essentially moral arguments against nuclear weapons, they have also been bolstered by academic research that suggested serious difficulties with idea that nuclear deterrence prevented war between the cold war superpowers. Towards the end of the cold war, John Mueller had argued that nuclear weapons and deterrence were irrelevant to the post-Second World War international stability, though he also argued that nuclear weapons do not fundamentally threaten stability either thus, disagreeing also with those who wanted nuclear abolition.[6] Others such as Bruce Blair pointed out to several instances of nuclear weapons accidents to suggest that if nuclear weapons use did not happen during the Cold War, this was more due to providence than any indication of the working of the hidden hand of nuclear deterrence.[7] Taking that argument further, Scott Sagan suggested organizational reasons why nuclear accidents are likely to happen.[8] Such arguments about the potential dangers

[4] George P. Schultz, William J. Perry, Henry A. Kissinger and Sam Nunn, 'A World Free of Nuclear Weapons,"*The Wall Street Journal*, January 4, 2007, p. A15.

[5] C.A.J. Coady, "Escaping from the Bomb: Immoral Deterrence and the Problem of Extrication," in Henry Shue (editor), *Nuclear Deterrence and Moral Restraint* (New York: Cambridge University Press, 1989) pp. 163-226.

[6] John Mueller, "The Essential Irrelevance of Nuclear Weapons: Stability in the Post-war World,"*International Security* 13:2 (Fall 1988), pp. 55.

[7] Bruce G. Blair, *The Logic of Accidental Nuclear War* (Washington: Brookings Institution, 1993)

[8] Scott D. Sagan, *The Limits of Safety: Organizations, Accidents and Nuclear Weapons* (Princeton: Princeton University Press, 1993)

posed by nuclear weapons, and at a more fundamental level the limits of nuclear deterrence logic, were reinforced by post-Cold War explorations of incidents of nuclear weapons accidents and crises such as the Cuban Missile Crisis, which illustrated how closely the two superpowers had come to actual nuclear weapon use.[9]

Such scepticism about nuclear deterrence has been extended to the argument that nuclear weapons in the hands of developing countries will be particularly dangerous. However, it must be noted here that even many scholars and analysts who argue that nuclear deterrence worked in the cold war and can work between the major nuclear powers (the nuclear five) appear convinced that the spread of nuclear weapons to the hands of new nuclear powers will likely increase the likelihood that nuclear weapons might be used in combat. In other words, there is great scepticism about whether nuclear deterrence will hold in cases of conflict between third world nuclear adversaries. Such 'proliferation pessimists' suggest a number of reasons why this is so: the 'irrational' nature of conflicts in the developing world; the unstable and unsettled nature of civil-military relations in these countries, the poor command and control systems available to new nuclear powers, the non-availability of safety systems such as permissive action links (PALs), are all cited as reasons why nuclear deterrence might fail in new nuclear nations.

As stated earlier, all those who argue that the spread of nuclear weapons will lead to deterrence failures are not all 'deterrence pessimists'. Some would argue that nuclear deterrence would

[9] Michael Dobbs, *One Minute to Midnight: Kennedy, Khrushchev and Castro on the Brink of Nuclear War* (New York: Alfred A. Knopf, 2008)

hold among established nuclear powers; their worry about the working of nuclear deterrence is confined to new nuclear powers. But some who make such arguments are deterrence pessimists who take the position that nuclear deterrence is unlikely to hold, whether between new nuclear adversaries or established nuclear powers. Such arguments at least have the benefit of consistency. Nevertheless, it is useful to note the contrasting position: following Kenneth Waltz's seminal essay in Adephi Paper No. 171, a whole group of scholars have argued that the principles of nuclear deterrence have universal validity, and that it is just as likely to hold among new nuclear adversaries as old.[10]

The problem with both these approaches – of either ignoring the logic of nuclear deterrence or of rejecting that logic – is that nuclear disarmament advocates have not been able to adequately address the key practical problem that decision-makers of nuclear armed states face: what are the consequences of giving up nuclear weapons and the deterrence benefits that are seen to flow out of the possession of nuclear weapons? The first position, of ignoring nuclear deterrence, obviously does not even address this problem, which makes it easy to understand why proposals for nuclear disarmament based on this position have never had any credibility. Unfortunately, until recently, most proposals were of this nature. The second position is somewhat more credible in pointing out that the benefits of nuclear deterrence might be overstated and the dangers inherent in nuclear weapons somewhat understated. Nevertheless, even this position does not fully address how states might address the issue of deterrence benefits because, in essence,

---

[10] Kenneth N. Waltz, *The Spread of Nuclear Weapons: More May Be Better*, Adelphi Paper No. 171 (London: International Institute for Strategic Studies, 1981)

it suggests the need to weigh these limited benefits against the potential dangers.

Taking Deterrence Seriously: Two Recent Proposals

Fortunately, at least some recent disarmament proposals claim to have taken the issue of nuclear deterrence more seriously. Below, the proposals, by Scott Sagan and Perkovich and Acton are considered.

The first issue that both works consider is the need for dialogue. Both essays begin by asserting the need for dialogue between the Nuclear Weapon States (NWS) and the Non-nuclear Weapon States (NNWS). Both these essays are based on the assumption that such dialogue is needed to deal with the two key bargains in the NPT: provision of civil nuclear technology and progress on nuclear disarmament in exchange for NNWS refraining from seeking nuclear weapons. Perkovich and Acton argue that "What is needed now is for a conversation about disarmament to take place between officials and experts from non-nuclear-weapons states and those from nuclear-weapons states. There has not been such a conversation for a long time."[11] Sagan also sees one of the key problems in nuclear disarmament as the lack of dialogue between the NWS and the NNWS. He sees much of the current interest in nuclear disarmament (especially among former decision-makers and military leaders in NWS) as being driven by a variety of fears of nuclear proliferation: that NWS behaviour is signalling to NNWS that they too should acquire nuclear weapons; the fear of nuclear terrorism, and hence the need to reduce the quantity of fissile materials available; the

---

[11] Perkovich and Acton, *Abolishing Nuclear Weapons: a Debate*, p. 14.

potential for nuclear deterrence to fail in new nuclear nations; and that NNWS will not stay in the non-proliferation regime if NWS do not disarm.[12] The problem as Sagan sees it is that these discussions – and their counterpoints – are primarily being debated among leaders in the NWS, whereas what is needed is a "coordinated global effort of shared responsibilities between NWS and NNWS."[13]

Debate between the NWS and NNWS on such issues can hardly be opposed. Indeed, repeated calls especially from the NNWS for a global Nuclear Weapons Convention (NWC) have been getting more support at international disarmament forums. A recent assessment by the International Campaign to Abolish Nuclear Weapons (ICAN) suggests that 140 states have taken either a 'supportive' or 'very supportive' position on NWC, with only 30 characterised as 'sceptical'.[14] Similarly, there are also more calls for yet another United Nations Special Session on Disarmament (UNSSOD).[15] If it were to fructify, this would the fourth such session (UNSSOD-IV), after previous ones in 1978, 1982 and 1988.

But the assumption that dialogue has been lacking and such dialogue will resolve these difficulties is more problematic.

---

[12] Sagan, "Shar ed Responsibility,"p. 2.

[13] Sagan, "Shar ed Responsibility," p. 3.

[14] "Government positions on a nuclear weapons conv ention,"International Campaign to Abolish Nuclear Weapons (August 2010) at http://www.icanw.org/files/NWC-positions-August2010.pdf

[15] Beatrice Fihn, "The CD discusses its draft report and other matters . . . behind closed doors," at ht tp://www.reachingcriticalwill.org/political/cd/2010/reports.html#7sept

Obviously, there has been continuing dialogue in many different forums between NWS and NNWS, including at the NPT Review Conferences and the annual Preparatory Committee (PrepCom) meetings, at the Conference on Disarmament (CD), and at other UN meetings. The problem is not so much that there is no dialogue but that there are fundamental political disagreements about balancing the different obligations. To suggest that more dialogue will resolve the 12-year long deadlock in the CD, for example, is not particularly helpful. Though there is little alternative to dialogue on these issues, a more helpful approach might be to consider seriously the political and security constraints that states face, rather than assume that states are simply being obstinate. Perkovich and Acton do consider some of the key political objections to nuclear disarmament: conventional force imbalances, missile defences, regional security issues, extended deterrence commitments and nuclear terrorism. But their suggestions to deal with some of these problems are neither practical nor are they likely to be effective. For example, on the issue of conventional force imbalances, they point out U.S. conventional force superiority may be a concern to Russia and China and other states. This is one of the key problems in dealing with nuclear disarmament and an issue that needs to be addressed if any progress is to be made. Unfortunately, Perkovich and Acton's suggestion, that the U.S. should reassure others, is likely to lead to more controversy. What should such reassurance include? Will the US cut its conventional military forces, and if so, which part of its force would be cut? Would military budgets be cut? What constitutes military budgets? Reassurance requires answering these and a multitude other questions. Unfortunately, Perkovich and Acton do not consider these issues and Sagan does not even raise the issue.

Another major issue relates to extended deterrence commitments that the US has given to its allies. Some have argued that US extended deterrence commitments make it difficult for the US to consider nuclear disarmament. Though Perkovich and Acton deal with the subject, they mainly suggest that the US needs to keep its allies such as the Europeans and the Japanese in the loop on progress being made towards nuclear disarmament. In addition they suggest that US conventional forces could provide the necessary commitment to keep its allies protected in a non-nuclear world. While this might be fine from Washington's perspective, it is unlikely that allies such as Japan, who live in less secure neighbourhoods will be satisfied. In addition, this suggestion points to a contradiction: if US is going to maintain conventional forces in other parts of the world in sufficient strength to provide extended conventional deterrence to its allies, would states like China and Russia agree to reduce their nuclear arsenals? Such a proposal might go directly against the suggestion that the US needs to 'reassure' other nuclear powers that nuclear disarmament will not lead to strengthening US conventional military lead over others. Sagan, on the other hand, disagrees that Washington's extended deterrence commitments is a hindrance to nuclear disarmament.[16] He suggests that there are two different kinds of extended deterrence commitments: one in which the US protects its allies from conventional as well as nuclear and other WMD threats, and another in which the US nuclear 'umbrella' (incidentally, a term he disagrees with) is used only to protect its allies from nuclear threats. The former characterized US commitment during the Cold War. Sagan argues that there are a number of advantages in moving towards the

---

[16] Sagan, "Shared Responsibility," p. 8.

latter posture: first, it supports those allies "who continue to value allied conventional military commitments, but feel that first-use nuclear threats encourage nuclear proliferation elsewhere in the world." Second, it makes US nuclear policy consistent with its own Negative Security Assurance (NSA). Third, it could move the US from the current 'commitment trap' of using nuclear weapons to retaliate against chemical and biological weapons use.[17] Finally such a move could also signal US acceptance of the goal of eventual nuclear disarmament. But Sagan himself admits some serious problem in making such a shift: such a changed deterrence posture "will not be easily accepted by all allies, nor will it be easy to implement within military establishments."[18] Indeed, writing in response to the Sagan essay, Ambassador Yukio Satoh clearly disagrees with him, arguing that the US should maintain ambiguity about whether or not it will use nuclear weapons to counter a chemical or biological attack on allies such as Japan but also that consideration of the issue of extended nuclear deterrence needs to be seen in the light of regional security and regional military balances.[19] His concern about the threat that Japan faces from China and North Korea should be taken as an indicator of the complexity of the issue.

Finally, Sagan's suggestion about what is needed to achieve nuclear disarmament reflects the difficulties ahead: he provides a roadmap for NWS and NNWS to "share responsibilities for

---

[17] Sagan had made the 'commitment trap' argument earlier. See Scott D. Sagan, "The Commitment Trap: Why the United States Should Not Use Nuclear Theats to Deter B iological and Chemical W eapons A ttacks,"*International S ecurity*, 24:4 (Spring 2000), pp. 85-115.

[18] Sagan, "Shar ed Responsibility," p. 9.

[19] Y ukio Satoh, "On R ethinking Extended Deterrence, " in Sagan et al, *Shared Responsibilities for Nuclear Disarmament*, pp. 32-35.

designing a future nuclear-fuel cycle regime, rethinking extended deterrence, and addressing nuclear breakout dangers while simultaneously contributing to the eventual elimination of nuclear weapons."[20] But what Sagan provides ultimately is a list of prescriptions for both NWS and NNWS to follow, without addressing why it is that states do not follow them. Similarly, Perkovich and Acton provide various suggestions about how to proceed further, but such plans of action raise even more problems. For example, they recognize that regional conflicts such as those over Palestine, Kashmir and Taiwan (to name only a few) can affect the prospects for nuclear disarmament because states in the region see nuclear weapons as providing the much needed security. But they do not provide a way in which to overcome these political problems other than the hope that all of these conflicts are on the way to resolution.

International Politics, Nuclear Deterrence and Nuclear Disarmament

The international political context is rarely seriously addressed in works on nuclear disarmament. For example, Perkovich and Acton do not seriously consider the issue of the desirability of nuclear disarmament. As they argue, the debate that they seek is "about how complete nuclear disarmament could be achieved safely and securely, not whether it should be tried."[21] They largely ignore the desirability issue because they consider it to be fairly obvious and because they focus mostly on what they and many others consider to be a more serious issue: the issue of the feasibility of nuclear disarmament. Nevertheless, the desirability issue is an

---

[20] Sagan, "Shared Responsibility," p. 3.

[21] Perkovich and Acton, *Abolishing Nuclear Weapons: A Debate*, p. 16.

important one too. Though nuclear weapons represent serious potential dangers, these dangers need to be set against the possibility of significant instability and war in a non-nuclear world: is a stable nuclear order worse than an unstable and war-prone non-nuclear order? Obviously, answering this question would depend on how stable the nuclear order is and how war-prone a non-nuclear order might potentially be. Addressing this requires addressing international political conditions that determine war-proneness.

Similarly, it is common, even among people who take security concerns that drive nuclearization seriously, to assume that at least some countries are motivated not so much by security concerns as by reasons of prestige. For example, Bruno Tertrais argues that one of the reasons countries such as India seek nuclear weapons is for prestige and that reforming the UN Security Council might be one way of addressing such concerns.[22] This, of course, is an issue that Perkovich and Acton also address in their main essay, though they note a number of difficulties with giving such privilege to India, such as opposition from China and Pakistan for such proposals. Such difficulties lead them to suggest that tying global nuclear disarmament to the reform of the UN Security Council (which is itself a serious problem) "might overload both efforts."[23] The practical difficulties of opening up the issue of UN Security Council permanent membership is little appreciated in New Delhi, but is nevertheless a serious one. Thus, adding this to the already onerous task of nuclear disarmament

---

[22] Bruno T ertrais, "Advancing the Disarmament Debate: Common Gr ound and Open Questions," in P erkovich and Acton, *Abolishing Nuclear W eapons: a Debate*, p. 182.

[23] Perkovich and Acton, *Abolishing Nuclear Weapons: A Debate* , pp. 106-108.

might very well be a foolish approach that could stymie progress on both fronts, as Perkovich and Acton point out.

But a far more serious problem is that such proposals tend to undermine and de-legitimise the security rationale for nuclear weapons for various states, especially in the developing world. Prestige is a part motive for either seeking or insisting on keeping nuclear weapons for all nuclear weapon states, including the very first nuclear weapon power, the U.S. For Russia, with an economy and standard of living that was barely above third world levels, nuclear weapons represented a key marker to its identity as a superpower during the Cold War period and as a major power in the post-Cold War period. Similarly for China nuclear weapons symbolized "China's prestige and international status as a great power."[24] This was true for the other two nuclear weapon powers too, the British and the French. Even for Pakistan, though the security motivation was a strong and primary factor, "the rhetoric that Pakistan was the first Muslim country to acquire nuclear weapons remains popular in the domestic political culture of Pakistan."[25] Prestige was at least one driver in the decision to acquire nuclear weapons for almost all the current nuclear-armed states, with the possible exception of Israel.But, for all these powers, security was an important factor too. The Soviet Union was threatened by American refusal to share nuclear technology; American nuclear threats were a key reason why China sought nuclear weapons. For smaller states such as Israel and Pakistan,

---

[24] Chu Shulong and Rong Yu, "China: Dynamic Minimum Deterrence," in Muthiah Alagappa, *The Long Shadow: Nuclear Weapons and Security in 21 st Century Asia* (Stanford, CA.: Stanford University Press, 2008), p. 161.

[25] Feroz Hassan Khan and P eter R. La voy, "P akistan: the Di lemma of Nuclear Deterrence," in Alagappa, *The Long Shadow*, p. 224.

security from larger and much more powerful adversaries could not be countered with conventional capabilities alone. For India, China represented a nuclear threat, though it was ultimately the advances that Islamabad made in its nuclear weapons programme that made an Indian nuclear arsenal unavoidable. The point is that for all nuclear-armed states, security is an important motivation. States do not go to the expense, risk and difficulties involved with building nuclear weapons for reasons of prestige alone, though prestige may be one additional factor. The implication of this is that focusing on prestige, and seeking alternate means to providing that prestige without nuclear weapons such as through membership of the UN Security Council membership or other means, will be an unnecessary and fruitless diversion. Without addressing security issues seriously, nuclear disarmament proposals will not be effective.

The failure to address the security issue is partly the consequence of the difficulty of the task. But it is also partly related to the refusal to address political issues. The assumption that nuclear disarmament can be achieved if all parties work together sincerely is a common belief among nuclear disarmament activists. There is an unwillingness on the part of nuclear disarmament activists to consider the limitations imposed by international political conditions, especially the structural circumstances within which states find themselves, which constrains what steps states can take. In other words, instead of seeing the limits of state behaviour as imposed by the requirements of pride or prestige – which could be overcome – we need to consider the possibility that these limits might be much more rigid and less amenable to manipulation by leaders and decision-makers. Proposing steps that are beyond the capacity of states and leaders to take is foolish and unhelpful.

Understanding these limits allows us to define what is possible and undertake steps that are possible even within these constraints.

In National security, decision-making is the most critical task that faces all states. States exist in a condition that international political theorists generally characterize as anarchy. Anarchy, of course, does not mean chaos: as used in this context, anarchy simply means that states live in a realm in which there is no higher political authority that can provide protection or adjudicate disputes. There is no world government that can provide order, and no global police force that can enforce justice. The consequence is that states live in an environment that is characterized as a 'self-help system'. Each state is left to its own devices to protect itself as best it can or suffer the consequences. A consequence of such a self-help system is the constant insecurity that all states face. Dealing with that insecurity is the primary task that all states face because none of the other goods that states provide – health, development, education and so on – are possible if this basic condition of security is not met. States pursue security through two means: either they build military muscle to protect themselves or else they seek alliance with other states that face common threats. But alliances are always temporary and fickle: because allies are never dependable, states prefer to defend themselves. However, sometimes they simply are not strong enough to defend themselves, making alliances the only choice. This has important implications when we consider the implications of extended deterrence and the choices facing non-nuclear American allies that depend on America's extended deterrence commitments for protection.

As both the key proposals that are analysed here make clear, extended deterrence commitment represents one of the thorniest issues facing any serious proposal for nuclear disarmament.

Nuclear weapons are unique because they appear to fundamentally alter this condition of insecurity. The enormous destructive power of nuclear weapons has meant that even otherwise relatively weak states such as North Korea and Pakistan can achieve a measure of security parity in relation to their much stronger adversaries. For this reason, weaker nuclear-armed states are likely to be much more averse to giving up nuclear weapons than the stronger states such as the US. Indeed, it is easy for the US to give up nuclear weapons because its conventional military capability provides it with a measure of security. Weaker states, without that margin of error, will be loath to give up their hard-won capabilities. Unfortunately, much of the current focus remains on the strongest players, another consequence of the failure to take seriously the political context.

Conclusion

One wishes that nuclear weapons were never invented. But they exist, and their presence has fundamentally affected international politics in a manner that no other weapon in human history has. Getting rid of nuclear weapons may be a noble goal, but such efforts need to grapple with the revolutionary nature of nuclear weapons. Many efforts towards nuclear disarmament over the last six decades have been attempted as propaganda and they were designed to fail. But even sincere efforts have not gone very far because they have refused to take into consideration these political conditions. More importantly, nuclear disarmament might be difficult because, as Brad Roberts argues in a short response piece in the Perkovich and Acton volume, "the international political conditions that could enable abolition do not currently exist."[26]

---

[26] Brad Roberts, "On Order, Stability and Nuclear Abolition," in Perkovich and Acton, *Abolishing Nuclear Weapons: a Debate*, p. 166.

SUMMARY OF DISCUSSIONS

After each presentation, there was an open discussion on the issues broughtout. Some of the comments are summarised below.

Kanwal Sibal

Traditionally, India has been against the concept of nuclear deterrence; against nuclear weapons per se, which is one of the reasons why India did not develop its nuclear capability. Once India became a nuclear weapon state, there was an obligation if nothing else to calm world opinion by bringing out very quickly a nuclear doctrine that spells out the Indian view on deterrence – of credible minimum value. Europe of course has had a very different view of deterrence, as always. Again there is a problem here when you talk about EU perspective on deterrence, I can't think of an EU perspective per se because the EU is not the nuclear authority in the European Union. Britain and France, the nuclear powers have their own view on nuclear deterrence, and the EU as a whole. First membership of NATO and hence the US nuclear umbrella may have a certain view on the working of the philosophy of deterrence during the cold war. Second, at the academic level all experts discuss deterrence not just as politics and military power. The problem is further confused by the fact that the EU has expanded and there are now members of the EU who were earlier part of the Warsaw Pact, who were aligned to the Soviet Union and who now have a very different persona. Nevertheless, since Britain and France have been nuclear weapon states and they have had their own view of what their nuclear weapons were meant to serve in terms of their security, it would perhaps in a sense will help us better understand what the European Union perspective is in the context of what the British and French views today are in their nuclear weaponry.

In an examination of the history of the European Union, not by itself, but in the broader ambit of its relationship with the United States and NATO, it is pertinent to note that the Atlantic Alliance did not believe in a minimum credible nuclear deterrent. On the contrary, they believed in massive arsenals which went up to 40000 nuclear weapons each, and which today remain at about 20,000. Contrary to our nuclear doctrine, the NATO alliance as well as Britain and France, have never believed in 'no first use' and continue to oppose any such proposal from non-nuclear weapon states, including a fresh nuclear weapon state like India.

On the question of tactical nuclear weapons, they do not form part of the Indian nuclear deterrent but certainly formed an integral part of the Atlantic deterrent and these tactical weapons have been stored on European soil, and even today remain there. At another level, the European concept of deterrence with UK and France forming the central pivots in fashioning the concept, was not an independent one. India's is an independent deterrent even if it is in the making, but theirs was never really an independent deterrent. In the case of UK, its nuclear arsenal was

US-dependent in some ways. For France it was inconceivable that it could in any conflict situation use nuclear weapons independent of NATO and independent of any decision that the United States may take. The U.S. would have been extremely averse to any of its European alliance partners trigging off a nuclear exchange with the Soviet Union in a situation where the United States did not feel that its core interests were involved.

The other difference is now visible in terms of a substantial reduction of the British and French nuclear arsenals. They have removed their land-based missiles, France still retains some air capability in this regard but essentially they are relying on submarine based nuclear weapons. In the case of India, our nuclear deterrent includes land based missiles and air delivered weapons as well as developing a submarine based capability, which is no longer the case of the European powers. Another difference is of India's geo-political situation is being entirely different from that of the European Union. Its two nuclear neighbours and relations between them is adversarial and these two countries collaborate with each other. Thus, India has to develop a minimum credible deterrent that has to take into account these challenges, which certainly the European Union is no longer facing with the end of the Cold War. While India is facing a situation of expanding nuclear arsenals on its borders, the European Union is actually facing a situation of contracting their nuclear arsenals, and Russia is very much part of the reduction process along with the United States. There is also a clear contrast in that the anti-ballistic missile systems which the United States had tried to install in the Czech Republic and in Poland, which in the Russian perspective is linked very much to the whole nuclear equation with USA. This is a complicating factor in Europe-Russia or NATO-Russia relationship, whereas this problem has not surfaced in the same way in so far as India is concerned.

Finally, nuclear deterrence cannot be viewed singly, but rather in the larger perspective of disarmament. Indian commitment to nuclear disarmament remains. A large body of Indian opinion still believes that ultimately the best thing is to move towards nuclear disarmament and in the interim take some steps towards which could be no-first use, which could also be delegitimisation of nuclear weapons in one way or the other. This rationale has been bought by Europe; certainly it has not been bought by France and Britain.

K. Subrahmanyam

In the year 2010, looking beyond the concept of non-proliferation, the most significant event has not been the NPT Review Conference, but the 46-nation Nuclear Security Summit convened by U.S. President Obama. The Obama declaration that came about was not contradicted by any of the heads of government and states present at the summit. The statement was about the irony that after the end of the Cold War, the chances of a nuclear confrontation between states has come down, while the chances of a nuclear attack has increased. In fact, in one statement, President Obama took away much of the significance of the review conference because the review conference was discussing calibration among the states with reference to inter-state confrontation. He was emphasizing that nuclear weapons are unlikely to be used by one state to threaten another state. What has happened since the Non-proliferation Treaty came into force can be viewed in a new light. New nuclear weapons states have come into being. Israel is not involved in any proliferation because Israel was a nuclear weapon state even when the Treaty was being formulated. India was a unique case which came in nuclear capability in 1974. There has been considerable proliferation to Pakistan and now North Korea. There is now a fear that it might spread to Iran. And in between we had one proliferation which got de-proliferated and that was the apartheid regime in South Africa. But if you take these four cases of proliferation, South Africa, Pakistan, North Korea and Iran, they were all states with inadequate legitimacy and acquired nuclear weapons not to fight nuclear wars, rather to shield themselves from externally induced regime change. In fact, there is one more state, which of late has been reportedly trying to acquire nuclear weapons and that is Myanmar.

Therefore, the idea that countries acquire nuclear weapons in order to fight nuclear wars is outdated. So also is the concept that nuclear wars are fightable today. Like the global financial crisis that arose not merely due to financial transactions but because the various institutions went to financial derivates wherein the case of derivatives and transactions involving derivatives, that the crisis arose. Similarly, it is not just the nuclear weapon itself but its derivative which is causing problems and creating a crisis. What is that derivative? Some of these regimes with inadequate legitimacy that have acquired nuclear weapons and are confident of having shielded themselves against pressures of regime change use, terrorism as instruments of state policy. This is a derivative of nuclear weapons, and countries like North Korea, Pakistan and Iran have been practicioning it. Of course, in the case of South Africa, once they transited from illegitimacy to legitimacy they gave up the nuclear weapons.

There is a need to view proliferation in a new fashion, and that is not being addressed or recognised. Proliferation came about by the idea of a proliferating state whose legitimacy was not questionable-China. In 1976, the Chinese decided to proliferate to Pakistan, and before that Mao Tse Tung had a principle that all peace loving states were entitled to have nuclear weapons. In 1982, Chinese Premier Deng Xiaoping opted for selective proliferation to three states.

The real nuclear issue is what has happened to North Korea, Pakistan or what is happening to Iran and what is likely to happen to Saudi Arabia. One may say nuclear weapons are not a weapon of war and that it is an instrument of terror. Consequently, a derivative of that can also, terrorism is also a derivative, is logical. And that is the main use which is being applied used against Europe. Today the threat that Europe faces is not from Russia, but terrorism that emanates from a nuclear shielded country which uses terrorism as its instrument of power. These are the issues that India should be raising. Thus, until the time major weapons powers keep their nuclear weapons, there is a fear of punitive reprisal in restraining rogue states like Pakistan or North Korea, for instance. Proliferation ought to be curbed before disarmament initiatives come into force that is the new reality of the world.

C. Raja Mohan

In terms of a state policy towards nuclear weapons, towards nuclear arms control and towards nuclear disarmament, India's policy has significantly evolved. It has evolved in a positive direction, but I think it needs to evolve some more to be able to contribute more actively in structuring a new international order.

In the Vedas there is *Smriti* and *Shruti*. The latter is the original thing that we memorise and it gets passed on from generation to generation irrespective of its meaning. *Smriti* is what you remember of the original mantra and the improvisations to it from time to time. It is often claimed that India has never signed a discriminatory treaty. What about the PTBT? India was the first to sign it without any urging to do so from the Americans.

Discrimination is the central argument that India raises regularly. I don't think we have taken a contract to end discrimination in the international system. India is worried about discrimination against itself. Once India is integrated into the non-proliferation system, it will be quite happy, to use Jaswant Singh's original famous phrase, —(having got into the train)— shut the compartment door against others coming in—. Iran is using this argument today that the NPT is a discriminatory one and Article IV is being circumscribed so that it cannot get nuclear enrichment technology. Tomorrow if Bangladesh uses the same argument and receives Chinese support will India insist on a non-discriminatory approach? Or are we going to say that a such a move will hurt our security interests. So therefore I think we need to move out of that mind set. The real issue for us is what should be our attitude towards non –proliferation and disarmament. I think as India's position moves from being defensive and fearful of the global regime to one reflecting its status as the third largest economy with significant military capabilities it will become its responsibility to support non-proliferation systems. It will be within our rights to support a discriminatory NPT because I would rather have a discriminatory NPT, than total anarchy.

Therefore, the challenge for India is how do we produce order? Are we thinking of producing order as a rising power or are we going to merely complain about discrimination. I think that phase is over for us. The central issue is how can we be part of the management of the global system The second aspect is about nuclear zero. India must work with other powers wherever possible to produce a system of a significant reduction in arsenals and not make debate on the "end state" as a way of not doing anything. I have no doubt it will be discriminatory to some, but the question is, are we going to be part of those who are enforcing an order or are we going to be with those protesting the new order.

The last point is linked to the balance of power politics. The NPT system was itself a product of Soviet-American balance and how it got applied to structures in Central Europe and East Asia that Germany and Japan had to be denuclearized no matter what. In the coming decades the balance of our choices may be between a rising China and a declining US. What would then be in India's interest? Ideally a concerted move by all nuclear weapon states towards nuclear zero.

However if there is in future a confrontation between the US and China, or that China extends nuclear deterrence to Pakistan or to some of India's neighbours, then we are talking about a completely different world in which we may to go in alliance with one set of nuclear powers against another set of nuclear powers. I think we are mentally not prepared for that and I think our challenge is to prepare for that world order where there is radical redistribution of power.

Harald Müller

Let me just immediately react to the article that you were quoting. I suppose it was a British or an American author and because usually British and American authors get it wrong when they write about either the European union or the German foreign policy applying very much a 19th century mindset to 21st century problems. There is continuity in German policy. Since Willy Brandt's Ostpolitik started in 1969, it has been the line of German policy to see to it that the Soviet Union, and later Russia, was embraced and integrated into the overall all-European polity, rather than confronted and thrown out. The idea is that there is calmness and peace in Europe by working with the Russians, and not against them all the while holding our powder dry just in case. That was the philosophy of Ostpolitik and, such is the philosophy which prevails today. Germany sees chances with the accession to power of President Medvedev, who by being a political find of former president Putin, is developing a slightly different profile which offer openings that can be further explored. That is the first thing.

Secondly, in terms of the energy dependency of Western Europe and Germany, particularly on Russia, the first controversy on that issue emerged in 1962 between Europe, Germany in particular and the United States on the building of a huge pipeline between the Soviet Union and Germany. At that time Germany gave up because of the pressure, followed by a rehearsal of the same in 1982-83 under President Reagan. Another pipeline, this time the French and the British sided with the Germans and the pipeline was built. Apparently the third coming of that issue is apparent now, all the while the Russian input into the German energy system never surpassed 10-15% given the internities, that is manageable. And it will remain so in the foreseeable future.

Thus, the situation is very much status quoist and a continuity of the past. And the fact that Germany leans towards French and Polish in this context is a rather natural move, for both are immediate neighbours, both are in the European Union, both are important partners for Germany. And, those are the ones with whom Germany want to see eye to eye on the major political issues.

With the French of course, Geremany had close consultation on foreign policy and security issues ever since the Elysee Treaty signed in the early 60's between Conrad Adenauer and Charles De Gaulle. Germany adheres to it because as long as France and Germany are living in peace in Europe, Europe would be in peace. Poland remains Germany's most important partner in Eastern Europe. The accession of Poland to both NATO and the European Union has enhanced German security tremendously. There are ghosts of the past which are still around which is no surprise.

European cooperation on non-proliferation initially was kept secret because the French and the British did not want to give the impression to the world that at the European level there was any authority of German competence, or even coordination on any issue that concerned security which was excluded from the Rome Treaties from the beginning. So the non-proliferation policy of the European Union actually started in 1991 with the establishment of a coordination group that was out of the sight of the public. It was only in 1984 that the surprised public got a glimpse of what was going on when the European council all of a sudden issued a statement on non-proliferation, specifically on the particular issue of nuclear exports and export controls. The trouble at that point of time was that a number of European member states were in the NSG, and were thus obliged to control at their borders nuclear transfers. At the same time they were members of EURATOM which obliged them not to have any export controls on nuclear items whatsoever. The first non-proliferation task of the European council was to reconcile these two sets of obligations, which finally happened through the accession of all members of the European Union to the NSG, which then solved the problem.

In 1986, a common European foreign policy was installed by a single European act and so the whole process got a legal and institutional underpinning, which was further refined and strengthened through the Maastricht and Amsterdam, and later, Lisbon Treaties. Step by step the entire foreign policy, of which non-proliferation was an increasingly important part, was becoming legalised and institutionalised. At present there is a sophisticated system with a double structure working through the committee on non-proliferation, another working through committee on disarmament in the United Nations. These two groups basically coordinate, as far as it is possible, positions on these issues of nuclear proliferation and nuclear disarmament inside the European Union. It helps to understand how these things develop further under the Lisbon Treaty which gave the foreign policy of the European union a more stable structure by appointing a virtual Foreign Minister for the Union who would be supported by a European foreign service that is to become operational from January 1st 2011. After a long struggle between the Commission and the Council Secretariat, it would be under the council's purview and as a corollory, non-proliferation policy may become more professionalised with the Foreign Service behind it.

The diversity of the European membership is a point that has to be emphasised. With nuclear weapon states, two of them, one of which has integrated its nuclear weapons into NATO, the other one reintegrated its conventional forces back to NATO, but not the nuclear forces, which in the French system are absolutely independent and completely under national control and not at the disposition of the Western Alliance. Then there is the alliance of 25 non-nuclear weapon states of very different convictions. About a third of them are NATO members, not more than that, almost half are NATO members and not all of them have nuclear weapons on their soil. Italy, the Netherlands, Belgium and Germany possesses nuclear weapons on its soil, which are in American custody. Some of them are supposed to be carried to the target whatever it might be by American aircraft, some of them are supposed to be carried to the target by the aircraft of the host country. The German, Belgian and Dutch Government's have indicated an interest in changing that arrangement. Germany would prefer these weapons to be removed from Europe and from its territory but of course in consensus with its NATO allies. In the eastern part of Europe there are member states who have a keener sense of a potential threat still residing from Russia. They want to be cautious on how to deal with these weapons and it revolves on the merit of the EU's Polish partners that a joint position has emerged in the last three quarters of the year, that the removal of these weapons must come in the course of some arms control agreement and arrangement with Russia. This is in fact being worked out at the NATO level.

The European non-proliferation policy emerged from the NPT review in 1990. During the conference in 1995, there was a joint action which is one of the formal instruments of common foreign and security policy with a view to extend the treaty definitely. In the year 2000, the Europeans managed to get a considerable part of the language they had prepared in a common position of all the member states into the final document of that conference, including language on disarmament of tactical nuclear weapons. In 2005, the apparent consensus basically disappeared because France partenered with the Bush administration on the crucial issue of whether the agreements on nuclear disarmament from the 2000 Review Conference were still valid or not. In the European common position this validity was reconfirmed, but in the French national position this validity was denied. And as a consequence, most of the time during that review conference the European Union was not an effective actor.

The European Union managed to get over the procedural hurdles which had nagged the conference for three weeks. The year 2003 might have been a turning point when the Europeans adopted for the first time a European security strategy and a European non-proliferation strategy with a concomitant action plan. This was in direct reaction to the deep split in the European Union over the Iraq war and the reaction to the United States security strategy of 2002. It was a document excelling in unilateralism in a way that even the British and some other European nations closer to the Bush administration,were sort of shocked and agreed that some sort of counterweight had to be formulated at the European level. If the two documents are compared with European and US security strategy of that time, one can observe the differences in the European emphasis on the importance of the Security Council, the importance of international law and multilateralism, and in particular, the need to have a Council mandate for all military action outside of self-defence, which of course relegated the Kosovo war to a historical exception. And the same applies to the European non-proliferation strategy which was completely built around the non-proliferation treaty, and its multilateral setting emphasised the role of the United Nations Security Council in enforcement, as opposed to unilateral enforcement based on national decisions.

Moreover, the action plan had about twenty individual items from funding the strengthening of nuclear security in the former Soviet Union to approaches to major non-aligned countries on non-proliferation. And that action plan has been amended year after year. The last amendment actually happened in June 2010 by the European Council and that has a rather strong emphasis on increasing consultation with important countries in the non-aligned movement that in terms of the accent it is setting, is sort of innovative. The Europeans of course have played not an unimportant role in the negotiations with Iran from 2003 and it should be re-emphasised that the initiative which was taken by Britain, France and Germany at that time was a very conscious reaction to the way the United States under the Bush administration had approached Iran. We saw at the time a great opportunity in the person of President Khatami and his group at the helm of the Iranian government, to overcome the deep risks and manage the cause of the Iranian nuclear programme. The negotiations were initially promising and they had stimulated and motivated President Khatami to make an absolutely unusual offer to Washington. But the whole process fell through because Washington was riding the high tide of regime change in Iraq, President Bush and his allies forced a regime change in Iran as well. They got one in 2005 but not in the direction they had preferred. Since then European diplomacy towards Iran was stalemating for Iran was playing a sophisticated well-orchestrated tactic to move very slowly closer to an option while taking offers, considering offers, making counter-proposals, then again turning the screw of its nuclear programme in another turn, and then follow up with another round of negotiations.

In the end the Europeans became convinced that it was impossible to strike a deal and very reluctantly moved to talks on stricter sanctions which initially Germany wanted to avoid. The trade volume between Germany and Iran is still between 4-5 billion Euros which for the German economy is not really important but at least it is some business which Germans are always reluctant to give up as good traders. Moreover, there is hardly an alternative. Even though the Europeans are such a diverse bunch, the fact that there is an operative non-proliferation policy even though much of that is at lower level, and a lot of that is not addressing the very big issue, is a model in itself.

2010 Jun NPT Rev-Con. -The Rev-Con started in a climate that was very different in 2005. The NPT is not a landmark but it stops the erosion of bilateral arms control and opens the possibility for additional steps. And it is also remarkable which has been hardly reported by the media that at the fringe of the Washington nuclear Summit under the aegies of President Obama, the Americans and the Russians signed an agreement that was lying idle for a decade on the safe disposition of weapons plutonium, 35 tonnes on either side under verification, which has been a troubling issue throughout the negotiations. The agreement is important because it might show the way for the future. How you deal in a verified way with weapons material? It may cast a long shadow on the disarmament process as it goes forward. This formed the atmosphere in which the review conference started with. The negotiations started as ever with the nuclear weapon states making nice remarks by showing reluctance in substance to go forward. The non-aligned movement making the best outrageous proposals for unacceptable moves forward and the business started in earnest. We had the formal negotiations in the three main committees and their three subsidiary bodies. We had from the beginning to the end bilaterals between the Egyptians and the Americans focussing on the Middle East. And we had from the end of the last but one week, small group negotiations of selected allegations selected by the president to formulate an action plan that would become the main result of the conference in case the main committee work would fall apart as it predictably did.

The Egyptians had one single goal that was to obtain strong language on the Middle East, to name Israel and to get some practical steps towards a Middle East nuclear weapon free zone. They played it by wearing the hat of the NAM speaker and taking very radical positions in that capacity, wearing the hat at the same time of the speaker for the new agenda coalition signalling in that capacity willingness to compromise. This was an unprecented move, and meanwhile negotiating all the time in the small group which met in the Egyptian embassy and with the Americans on the Middle East. They were marvellously capable leading the non-aligned in tandem with the Brazilians who for the first time played a major role in the conference. On the side of the nuclear weapon states, the willingness to give more was probably confined to the Americans. The Chinese wanted to be celebrated for all the good things they had done, notably declare 'no first use' while not moving an inch on anything else, notably on transparency. These factors shaped the negotiation game by which the non-aligned countries blocked any significant move forward for the non-proliferation toolbox, such as the additional protocol to the NPT as the binding verification standards, such as the recognition that export controls are duty of everybody and the NSG guidelines are a reasonable tool for moving some procedures on withdrawal stimulated of course by the experience of north Korea where the NPT community would react as a whole to a state announcing withdrawal from the treaty.

Everything fell by the wayside because the non-aligned countries blocked things as long as they did not get anything on nuclear disarmament, and the nuclear weapon states made only the most timid moves forward. There is some language on the qualitative improvement of nuclear weapons, the constraint of which is recognised as a legitimate interest of the non-nuclear weapon states. There is also some commitment by the nuclear weapon states not to circumvent the goals of the Comprehensive Test Ban Treaty by using new technology for developing new types of warheads. There was also some rhetoric on regular and systematic reporting on the nuclear arsenals and on disarmament. A commitment that all types of nuclear weapons independent of their location will be addressed in the regular disarmament process which includes implicitly the tactical nuclear weapons in Europe which is of considerable interest to Poland. Thus there was a consensus at the lowest minimum denominator. What stands as the result of this conference is the part on the Middle East where the Secretary General is invited to nominate/appoint a facilitator for preparing 2012 conference on a Middle East nuclear weapon free zone. All parties are committed to foster the goal of that conference and the conference will be held under United Nations auspices. It is appropriate to say that this is exerting strong pressure on Israel, which must consider how to deal with that. It is now on the agenda with the consent of all the permanent members of the Security Council, of all of the NPT community. That Israel was named in that final document was not only inevitable but also adequate. It is by now the only state in the Middle East that has nuclear weapons and is not a member of the NPT. The Israeli government has reacted with hostility to that proposition and we have to wait and see how things evolve over the next two years.

The outcome for the NPT, gave us some breathing space. While it did not strengthen the treaty, it just avoided weakening it further. The breathing space must be used to get much more unity into the treaty community to move forward on nuclear disarmament. If the breathing space is not utilised by the membership, the NPT will return to erosion with a revenge.

ABOUT THE CONTRIBUTORS

Rajesh Rajagopalan is Professor and Chair at the Centre for International Politics, Organization and Disarmament, School of International Studies, Jawaharlal Nehru University, India. Previously, he was Senior Fellow at the Observer Research Foundation, New Delhi, and Research Fellow at the Institute for Defence Studies and Analyses, New Delhi. He also served as Deputy Secretary in the National Security Council.

Ambassador Arundhati Ghose joined the Indian Foreign Service in 1963. She worked in various capacities in the Embassies of India and Permanent Representative of India to UN Offices in Geneva, and the Conference on Disarmament. She is on the editorial board of *Disarmament Times* (New York) and *Faultlines* (New Delhi). She has been writing on arms control issues including small arms.

Prof. Harald Mueller is Executive Director, Head of Research Department (RD) RD: Policies for Security Governance of States of the Peace Research Institute, Frankfurt. He is a consultant on arms control, disarmament and non-proliferation and German and American foreign and security policies.

Gurmeet Kanwal is Director, Centre for Land Warfare Studies, New Delhi. He was formerly Director Security Studies and Senior Fellow, Observer Research Foundation, New Delhi; Senior Fellow, Institute for Defence Studies and Analyses, New Delhi;

Senior Fellow, Centre for Air Power Studies, New Delhi and Visiting Research Scholar at the Cooperative Monitoring Centre, Sandia National Laboratories, USA.

Lukasz Kulesa is Acting Head of the Research office at the Polish Institute of International Affairs and analyst in the areas of nuclear non-proliferation, security policy of Poland and the future of NATO. He has co-authored several books and chapters, articles in reputed publications.

K. Subrahmanyam was a prominent international strategic affairs analyst, journalist and former Indian civil servant. Considered a proponent of *Realpolitik*, Subrahmanyam has long been an influential voice in Indian security affairs. He was most often referred to as the doyen of India's strategic affairs community, and as the premier ideological champion of India's nuclear deterrent.

Ambassador Kanwal Sibal joined the Indian Foreign Service in 1966. He reached the highest position in the India Foreign Service on his appointment as Foreign Secretary to the Government of India from July 2002 to November 2003. He was a member of India's National Security Advisory Board (November 2008 to November 2010). He is on the Board of Directors of the New York based East-West Institute and also on the Advisory Board of the Vivekananda International Foundation.